U.S.S. CONNECTICUT

CONSTITUTION STATE BATTLESHIP

TO

Please enjoy the read—

U.S.S. CONNECTICUT

CONSTITUTION STATE BATTLESHIP

MARK ALBERTSON

TATE PUBLISHING & *Enterprises*

TATE PUBLISHING
& Enterprises

Tate Publishing is committed to excellence in the publishing industry. Our staff of highly trained professionals, including editors, graphic designers, and marketing personnel, work together to produce the very finest books available. The company reflects the philosophy established by the founders, based on Psalms 68:11,

"THE LORD GAVE THE WORD AND GREAT WAS THE COMPANY OF THOSE WHO PUBLISHED IT."

If you would like further information, please contact us:

1.888.361.9473 | www.tatepublishing.com

TATE PUBLISHING & Enterprises, LLC | 127 E. Trade Center Terrace Mustang, Oklahoma 73064 USA

U.S.S. Connecticut: Constitution State Battleship

Cover design by Chris Webb
Interior design by Jennifer Redden

Published in the United States of America

ISBN: 978-1-5988673-9-8
07.05.06

Dedicated to the officers and bluejackets
who manned the decks of
Battleship Connecticut.

ACKNOWLEDGEMENTS

Most writers work in solitude. Yet there is not one who completes a book without assistance from others. Those who lend their support do so because they believe in the project. They also lend their support because of their confidence in the writer's ability to tell the story. I am no exception to this rule. I began the quest to commemorate the centennial of battleship *Connecticut* alone. But as I progressed, others appeared along the way who stepped forward to lend invaluable assistance.

First I would like to thank Michael Daly, managing editor of the Connecticut Post, for publishing my first article on battleship *Connecticut*. Next I would like to thank Senator Robert Duff of Connecticut's 25th Senate District, senatorial assistant Dean O'Brien and Representative Chris Perone of Connecticut's 137th Assembly District. Their efforts in helping to commemorate battleship *Connecticut* before both houses of the General Assembly in Hartford on May 25, 2005 is deeply appreciated. I would also like to thank all those at Tate Publishing, especially Miss Trinity Tate, acquisitions manager, and Dr. Richard Tate, co-founder of Tate Publishing, for their assistance in bringing the finished product to light. For this they have my undying gratitude.

Closer to home, I would like to thank John and Carmella Pagliano, whose support and affection make them more like parents than in-laws. To my mother, Alice Albertson, a gallant lady who has shown me on more than one occasion just what perseverance and fortitude can accomplish. To my late father, William Albertson, a World War II Navy vet. From "The Sailor" I inherited a desire to learn history and a respect for this nation's maritime tradition. To Mr. Frank DeBart, who at an early stage in my life, helped show me purpose and direction.

To my oldest son, Michael, and for the many years spent together as bowling partners, and for having enjoyed the unique good fortune of playing hockey together as father and son for five seasons. To my daughter Theresa, and for her incomparable gift of two wonderful granddaughters. And to my son, Erik; wherever this leatherneck is stationed, I hope he is as proud of this book as I am of his desire to serve this great country.

And last but certainly not least, to my wife, Rose Marie. This lovely lady is my biggest booster and biggest critic. But thank God for the best friend I ever had.

TABLE OF CONTENTS

PART THREE

PART FOUR

FOREWORD

Connecticut is a great state with a most wonderful and glorious history. From the days prior to being a nation, Connecticut was the benchmark for democracy, freedom and liberty. It was only fitting then that in 1907 the USS *Connecticut* would be the flagship for the country's "Great White Fleet."

In a first of its kind, around the world, show of strength symbolizing America's global dominance, the crew of *Connecticut* took its responsibility very seriously. Moreover, there was a keen understanding of the importance of their mission from a military and a symbolic point of view.

Mark Albertson has done an extraordinary job telling the story of the impressive ships that sailed more than 46,000 miles in the Atlantic and Pacific oceans. Not only is history captured in this book, but so is a sense of spirit and can-do attitude that comes from being an American.

I am very grateful for Mark's work in writing this book. He is a great citizen of this state and a true patriot. On behalf of Representative Chris Perone, Dean O'Brien and my colleagues in the Senate, our deepest gratitude for capturing this rich history and allowing others to share in our pride.

Senator Robert Duff
25th Senate District, State of Connecticut

PREFACE

I was once an avid modeler. I used to spend many relaxing hours building ships, planes, vehicles and guns. My favorites were ships, battleships in particular. *Arizona, Pennsylvania, Iowa, Bismarck, Tirpitz, Yamato, Musashi, King George V and Richelieu.* I built them, displayed them, or gave them away to friends, relatives, shut-ins, history buffs or anyone else who expressed interest in them. But the most rewarding aspect of the pastime was not in the construction of these marvelous vessels, but in capturing an important piece of history.

Battleships were the strategic weapons of their day. Their heyday ran from the mid-1890s through the First World War. Nations large and small built or bought battleships in pursuit of strategic agendas of regional or global significance. Great Britain and Germany set the pace. These two nations engaged in a dreadnought-building contest that foreshadowed the later Cold War competition in nuclear arms between the United States and the Soviet Union; a competition which pitted British quantity against German quality and culminated in a single afternoon in 1916 on the dreary seas off the Skagerrak.

The United States, too, was a contestant in the battle-ship-building competition. As an up and coming power eager to take its place under the sun, it had been recognized that sea power was a prerequisite for achieving the status of global power. And only with sea power was it possible to defend the overseas interests of a global power. Yet unlike Britain and Germany, which later engaged in a bloody free-for-all in the North Sea, the United States demonstrated its ability to project power with a more subtle yet unmistakable show of force. The round-the-world cruise of the Great White Fleet was not just another demonstration of naval power; rather, it was one of the greatest achievements in modern maritime history—the first major strategic initiative by the United States in the twentieth century. The Spanish-American War of 1898 introduced the United States to the ranks of the imperialist powers; but the triumph of the Great White Fleet made the United States a global power, and in so doing, set the stage for it to become a super power.

But the Great White Fleet was not made up of super battleships of the likes of *Iowa*, *Bismarck* or *Yamato*. It was made up of the pre-dreadnought type of capital ship. Ships which were less than 500 feet long, weighed less than 20,000 tons and had a top speed of under 20 knots. Unlike the dreadnoughts that carried a single major caliber of main armament, pre-dreadnoughts carried a mixed array of fire power in turrets or casemates along the hull. Crew complements generally totaled no more than 1,000 officers and ratings. There was no radar or sonar, and wireless transmission was in its infancy.

Pre-dreadnoughts burned coal. Unlike oil, which was pumped through hoses from one ship to another, coaling was a much more labor-intensive effort. From a collier's hold to a battleship's bunker, dirty, sweaty bluejackets manhandled ton after ton of the dusty, black cinders. Eyes and lungs became clogged. Arms, legs and backs ached. Ships had to be scruBBed clean, as coal dust settled everywhere like a springtime pollen in New England. It is indeed truly amazing that these dirty, sooty coal-burners could actually cross the Atlantic or the Pacific, let alone circumnavigate the globe. But circumnavigate the globe they did, sixteen of them, steaming a remarkable 46,000 miles.

The flagship of the Great White Fleet was battleship *Connecticut*. Battleship *Connecticut* was the lead ship of a class of six, the largest single class of battleship ever produced by the United States. The *Connecticuts* were the epitome of American pre-dreadnought design, and five of the six ships made the trip with the Great White Fleet. Battleship *Connecticut* was the only battleship to ever represent the Constitution State on the Navy roster and was the fourth of five warships to be named Connecticut. Like her sisters, battleship *Connecticut* served the United States nobly in peacetime and in war.

I never built a model of battleship *Connecticut*. And to the best of my knowledge, not one of the major modeling companies markets the vessel. However, in the course of my research, I have come to know this vessel better than any other battleship I ever read about or displayed as a model. And I hope with this book I have captured the true essence of this historic warship more so than if I had put it to glue and plastic.

Many books and publications have catered to the later dreadnoughts and fast battleships. But sadly, the pre-dreadnoughts like *Connecticut* have been largely ignored. USS *Connecticut: Constitution State Battleship* seeks to address this issue, even if only in a small way. To the people of the State of Connecticut, it is important for them to remember that the battleship named after their state led an endeavor that changed the world, and did so without firing a single shot in anger. For historians, maritime enthusiasts and history buffs, I hope they find USS *Connecticut: Constitution State Battleship* a welcome addition to the maritime history of early twentieth century America.

INTRODUCTION

On December 11, 1998 at Groton, Connecticut, a new warship was commissioned into the fleet. SSN22 was the second of three *Seawolf* class attack submarines and the fifth warship in the history of the United States Navy to bear the name USS *Connecticut*.

USS *Connecticut* is the most advanced attack submarine in the world. Stretching more than 350 feet long and tipping the scales at more than 9,100 submerged tons, SSN22 is capable of speeds in excess of 35 knots and depths greater than 1,600 feet. *Connecticut* boasts a formidable array of weaponry ranging from cruise missiles and torpedoes to mines and anti-ship missiles. Total complement is 133 officers and men.

At home or abroad, USS *Connecticut* plays an integral role in the strategic defense of the United States. *Connecti-*

cut's importance to the Navy at the dawning of the twenty-first century is not too unlike that of her predecessor of one hundred years before. Battleship *Connecticut* was then an important part of America's first line of defense.

Yet a warship is only as effective as its ability to project power. For SSN22, this ability is based on stealth and superior technology. For battleship *Connecticut*, it meant big guns and armor plate. Yet the objective was the same: command of the seas. Command of the seas is just as important to America's survival as a global power today as it was a century ago. And no one understood this concept any better than that committed navalist Theodore Roosevelt.

In 1907, the president was eager to demonstrate America's ability to project power from the Atlantic to the Pacific in time of crisis. What he originally had intended as a subtle show of force gradually became a full-fledged demonstration of naval power. A display intended to not only show the flag worldwide, but to instill in Americans a sense of pride in their navy.

On December 16, 1907, the Atlantic Fleet Battleship Force weighed anchor and departed Hampton Roads. During the next fourteen months, sixteen coal-burning battleships, forever known as the Great White Fleet, steamed more than 46,000 miles in circumnavigation of the globe: an extraordinary peacetime demonstration of naval power that generated incalculable goodwill and sowed the seeds of strategic alignments that would later pay priceless dividends in two world wars.

And the name of the flagship that led the way on this monumental maritime achievement? Why, none other than USS *Connecticut.*

PART ONE

THE PREDECESSORS

THE FIRST WARSHIP NAMED CONNECTICUT

The first *Connecticut* was built in Skenesborough, New York, in 1776. She was a gondola armed with one 12-pounder, two 8-pounders, eight swivel guns and a crew of 45 men. *Connecticut* was under the command of Captain Grant of the Continental Army and attached to Brigadier-General Benedict Arnold's fleet in Lake Champlain.

In June, the Americans had evacuated Canada. The British planned to follow up the colonial's retreat with an offensive through the Adirondacks. The invasion route was to be the Lake Champlain—Lake George—Hudson River axis. The objective was to wrest control of the Hudson Valley, thereby cutting off the New England states from the rest of the colonies.

On October 11, 1776, General Arnold's fifteen-ship task

force, which included *Connecticut*, engaged a British fleet several times its size. From sunrise to sunset, the opposing fleets slugged it out off Valcour Island. Outnumbered and outgunned, Arnold withdrew with four ships heavily damaged. The next day, *Connecticut*, pursued by British warships, attempted to escape up an inlet near Crown Point. With their position hopeless, the crew set fire to *Connecticut* to prevent her capture and then retired on foot.

The sacrifice of *Connecticut* and the pluck of Arnold's fleet prevented the British from consolidating their victory. Winter was fast approaching, and soon Lake Champlain, Lake George and the Hudson River would be choked by ice. The planned British offensive was put off until the following summer. However, the year's delay proved costly. On October 17, 1777, the Continental Army of General Gates defeated the Redcoats of British General Burgoyne at Saratoga. The result was an alliance with France, an association that would eventually help the colonists defeat the British forces. *Connecticut* and the other ships of Benedict Arnold's fleet helped to put the British off their timetable and played a prominent role in preserving the Revolution.

THE SECOND WARSHIP NAMED CONNECTICUT

The second *Connecticut* was launched June 6, 1799 in Middletown, Connecticut. The man-of-war displaced 492 tons and bristled with twenty-six 12-pounder guns. Her complement totaled 180 seamen. Captain Moses Tryon was placed in command. On October 15, *Connecticut* headed for the Caribbean to begin a brief but gallant career in the war against pirates.

Connecticut was attached to the command of Richard V. Morris at Guadalupe Station. The new arrival went into action straightway. On November 6, Captain Tryon and his crew recaptured the American schooner *Hannah*. The following month, the American brig *Penelope* was recovered, and the schooner *Polly* was forced aground and destroyed on Guadalupe Island.

Speed proved a valuable asset in running down the elusive pirates. And *Connecticut* became renown throughout the Caribbean for her swiftness. On December 29, 1799, her speed played a vital role in ending the career of one of the most notorious pirate ships of the day, the sixteen-gun *Italia Conquese*. In four years, this French privateer had destroyed or captured 150 vessels. In a spirited exchange of gunfire, *Connecticut* shot away the Frenchman's rigging, then raked her topsides with withering fire. The renegade's colors were hauled down, and the vessel was captured.

On January 14, 1800, off Desrada Island, the scrappy *Connecticut* exchanged gunfire with a French schooner, then took on a 22-gun French vessel ferrying wine and plate from Bordeaux. The vessel was run aground and destroyed by the Yankee man-of-war.

For the next six weeks, *Connecticut* patrolled Puerto Rican waters before returning to Guadalupe. On March 20, *Connecticut*, in concert with frigate *Adams*, recaptured the American schooner *Priscilla* and her cargo of flour, beef and pork. On April 27, the *Thomas Chalky* out of Philadelphia was recaptured.

By June 1, *Connecticut* was again prowling the waters off Desrada when she overhauled the French privateer *Le Piege*. Two days later, she liberated *Martha and Mary* from the clutches of the French. This American brig was out of Baltimore with 800 barrels of flour and 20,000 shingles.

On June 5, *Connecticut's* speed proved decisive in her next enemy action. *Connecticut* traded shots with the French privateer *La Unite*. Outgunned, the Frenchman broke off and fled with *Connecticut* in hot pursuit. The chase lasted twelve hours, with the pirate crew throwing overboard guns, ammunition and anything else not nailed down in a vain attempt to gain more speed. Nevertheless, the schooner was overhauled and taken in prize. *Connecticut* escorted the captive back to St. Kitts.

Connecticut's last action occurred on July 15, 1800 when she captured the privateer *Le Chou Chou*. She was then ordered stateside. *Connecticut* returned to New London on October 19. Captain Tryon turned over command to Captain Richard Derby. Captain Derby was to see to *Connecticut's* refit for her new assignment in Batavia (Jakarta), to protect American shipping in the East Indies. However, deployment was canceled when the Treaty of Friendship with France was ratified by Congress. On April 1, 1801, Captain Derby sailed *Connecticut* out of New London for New York. The gallant warship's career ended ingloriously at public auction when she was sold for $19,300.

THE THIRD WARSHIP NAMED CONNECTICUT

The third *Connecticut* was built in 1861 by William WEBB. The Navy purchased the vessel on August 18, 1861 and commissioned her at the New York Navy Yard on August 23, 1861. Commander Maxwell Woodhull assumed command.

This version of *Connecticut* was a steamer. She measured 251 feet 6 inches in length and had a beam of 38 feet 2 inches. Top speed was 10 knots. The crew totaled 166 officers and men. Armament consisted of four 32-pounder guns and one 12-pounder.

Connecticut departed New York on August 25, 1861. Her holds were crammed with men, coal and stores for naval forces blockading Confederate ports. She called on Charleston, Savannah, Jupiter Inlet, Key West, Pensacola, the Mississippi River Delta and Galveston. On her return voyage, she stopped at Havana before returning to New York on September 18, 1861.

Connecticut underwent dockyard repairs in the New York Navy Yard. On November 10, 1861, she put to sea with supplies for Union blockading forces outside Port Royal, South Carolina. After discharging her supplies, she departed Port Royal for Galveston. Off the coast of Florida, *Connecticut* intercepted the blockade runners *Adeline* and *Dealander*. Both schooners were taken as prizes and escorted to Key West. *Connecticut* continued on to Galveston. Here she took on a load of sick and wounded and then departed the Texas port for New York, arriving December 17, 1861.

On January 7, 1862, *Connecticut* cleared New York Harbor for another trip loaded with supplies and stores for the blockading squadrons. Off Jupiter Inlet, *Connecticut* captured the blockade runner *Emma* and escorted the prize to Key West. By November, *Connecticut* made three more such supply cruises, all of which proved uneventful. However, during 1862, *Connecticut* was subject to a flurry of command changes. On June 29, Maxwell Woodhull was relieved by Commander Edward A. Barnett. Barnett in turn was relieved by Lieutenant H. Haxtun on August 21. Haxtun was succeeded on December 15 by Commander George W. Cooper.

On December 24, 1862, *Connecticut* steamed out of New York with ironclad *Montauk* in tow. The ironclad was left with blockading forces at Cape May. *Connecticut* spent the next six months as an escort, protecting Union steamers en route to Florida, Cuba and Panama. She returned to New York on June 6, 1863, for a much needed overhaul.

On August 4, Commander Cooper was reassigned and replaced by Commander John J. Almy. One week later, *Connecticut* was steaming south for Wilmington, Delaware, and eleven months of blockade duty.

On September 22, the blockade runner *Juno* was captured while bound for Bermuda. The following day, *Phantom* was intercepted. This renegade ran aground and was torched by its crew. *Connecticut* lowered a whaleboat of armed sailors who gave chase. Ashore, one of the bluejackets was killed in a gun battle with fleeing Confederates.

Connecticut went several months before her next prize, the *Sallie,* was taken on December 20. This was followed on March 1, 1864 by the *Scofia,* loaded with cotton. On May 9, *Minnie* was sighted. Four shots across the bow caused the Rebel steamer to heave to. Another cargo of cotton, tobacco and turpentine would not reach Bermuda. The next day, *Greyhound* was taken. Among her cotton and crew was a famous southern Belle of the day known as "Belle Boyd."

Connecticut broke off blockade duty on July 16, 1864 and

proceeded to the Boston Navy Yard for a much needed over-haul. Following her refit, *Connecticut* spent the next three months shuttling up and down the southern east coast and the Gulf, supplying men and stores to blockading squadrons. On October 5, 1864, she was back in Boston for another refit.

On February 17, 1865, Captain Charles G. Boggs assumed command. Four days later, *Connecticut* was at sea bound for Charleston. She arrived March 2, loosing a 21-gun salute in honor of the capture of the city. She departed Charleston on March 10 with supplies and dispatches for American diplomats in the CariBBean. She called on Santo Domingo, Puerto Rico, the Virgin Islands, Windward Islands, Barbadoes, Venezuela and Curacao, ending up at New Grenada on April 29. At the last named port, *Connecticut* fired a 21-gun salute in honor of the capture of Richmond and Lee's surrender.

Connecticut sallied for Aspinwall, Panama. While in Panama, Captain Boggs called the crew to muster and announced the death of President Lincoln. On May 21, *Connecticut* embarked, calling on Havana before arriving at Hampton Roads on May 24. Two days later, she was in Philadelphia.

In July, *Connecticut* made her final sortie. She towed the ironclad *Catskill* to Port Royal and then towed the steamer *Nabant* back to Philadelphia.

On August 3, 1865, *Connecticut* put back into the Philadelphia Navy Yard. Her colors were lowered for the last time on August 15. She was struck from the Navy roster and sold on September 21, 1865.

PART TWO

BATTLESHIP CONNECTICUT

EAST RIVER TO HAMPTON ROADS

On March 10, 1903, the keel was laid in the Brooklyn Navy Yard for the fourth warship to represent the Constitution State. USS *Connecticut* (BB-18) was the lead ship of a class of six, followed by battleships USS *Louisiana* (BB-19), USS *Vermont* (BB-20), USS *Kansas* (BB-21), USS *Minnesota* (BB-22) and USS *New Hampshire* (BB-25).

USS *Connecticut* was launched on September 29, 1904. Miss Alice Welles, granddaughter of former Secretary of the Navy Gideon Welles, served as sponsor. Upwards of 30,000 people lined the East River to watch America's newest and most powerful battleship slide down the building ways. At the time of her launch, *Connecticut* was some fifty-five percent complete, with most of her upper works, protection, machinery and fire power to be installed. It would be two years before she was ready. And on September 29, 1906, USS *Connecticut* was commissioned in the New York Navy Yard. Captain William Swift, USN, assumed command.

The *Connecticuts* were an improvement over the previous five *Virginia* class battleships. The *Connecticuts* had a greater weight of hull, more protection and fire power. They were longer than their predecessors and, despite an additional 1,500 tons displacement, were able to achieve the same speed on reduced horsepower. With a greater bunker capacity, the *Connecticuts* could outrange the *Virginias* by 1,000 nautical miles at 10 knots.

BB-18 steamed out of New York on December 15, 1906. Her destination was the Virginia Capes, where Captain Swift put America's newest battleship through its paces in a variety of training exercises. On Christmas Day in Lynhaven Bay, the crew enjoyed a lavish holiday dinner. As an added attraction, a variety of house wines was served—a gift to the ship from the grateful citizens of the State of Connecticut.

Connecticut underwent shakedown training and took part in battle practice exercises with the fleet off Puerto Rico and Cuba. Upon conclusion, *Connecticut* steamed back to the United States, arriving at Hampton Roads on April 16, 1907. Rear Admiral Robley D. Evans, Commander-in-Chief United States Atlantic Fleet, transferred his flag from USS *Maine* (BB-10) to *Connecticut*. BB-18 was now flagship of the Atlantic Fleet. At the same time, there occurred a change in commanding officers, with Captain Hugo Osterhaus being piped aboard.

On April 25, 1907, President Theodore Roosevelt officially opened the Jamestown Exposition. Battleship *Connecticut* was named official host for vessels visiting from other nations. Admiral Evans joined President Roosevelt in conducting many of the ceremonies. Sailors and Marines from *Connecticut* took part in many events ashore. On April 29, the governors of Virginia and Rhode Island joined many foreign dignitaries for festivities aboard *Connecticut*. The Exposition concluded on May 4 on the quarterdeck of *Connecticut*, where Rear Admiral Evans, as master of ceremonies, conducted trophy presentations to the victors of the sailing races.

On June 10, 1907, *Connecticut* took part in the Presidential Fleet Review off Hampton Roads. Three days later, BB-18 was on her way to the New York Navy Yard for a scheduled overhaul. Following her refit, *Connecticut* was ordered north to take part in maneuvers off Massachusetts and Maine. During these exercises, *Connecticut* conducted standardization trials. On August 7, BB-18 made five full power runs, achieving a speed of 18.59 knots. Her best run was a sprint of 19.01 knots.

Connecticut steamed south for the Virginia Capes for

more maneuvers and then north once again for Cape Cod and target practice. On September 6, *Connecticut* was ordered back to the New York Navy Yard. She was slated for a refit for a most important duty; a duty which would become her greatest honor: flagship for the round-the-world cruise of President Theodore Roosevelt's Great White Fleet.

"You've Done the Trick!"

On December 5, 1907, USS *Connecticut* slipped her moorings and steamed out of New York Harbor. She arrived at Hampton Roads the next day. One by one, her sisters assembled with her until sixteen battleships had gathered at the Roads.

The following eight days were known as "Navy Farewell Week." The preparations and festivities concerning the fleet's departure were extensive. Every battleship took on coal, stores and ammunition to capacity. Officers and men were feted to a seemingly endless litany of receptions, luncheons, dances and balls. The finale occurred on Friday the 13th, a grand ball at the Chamberlin Hotel. The guests of honor were Admiral Evans and the officers of the squadron. The guest list of the formal affair represented a who's who of Washington D.C., Baltimore, Richmond and other eastern cities.

At 0800 hours, December 16, 1907, the Stars and Stripes went up every yardarm in the squadron. The presidential yacht *Mayflower* passed in review. On signal from *Connecticut,* sixteen gleaming white battlewagons loosed a 21-gun salute. President Roosevelt was overcome with the magnificence of the moment—pennants flying, bands blaring on every quarter deck, sailors and Marines topside on parade. He turned to Secretary of the Navy Victor H. Metcalf, and said, "Isn't it magnificent!"

Mayflower dropped anchor between *Vermont* and *Missouri.* Rear Admiral Evans, his divisional commanders and all battleship skippers were piped aboard *Mayflower* to pay their respects to the commander-in-chief. The president met with each and every man and took time for photographs. Afterwards the president met with Admiral Evans in private. Following the formalities, the officers were shuttled back to their commands.

At 1000 hours, *Mayflower* upped anchor and proceeded out of the Roads. On signal from Admiral Evans on board *Connecticut,* every battleship in his squadron weighed anchor and got up steam. *Connecticut's* screws began to churn the waters off Old Point Comfort. Ship by ship, division by division, the squadron fell astern the flagship. Sixteen plumes of thick black smoke marked the fleet's departure.

Mayflower waited at the Tail-of-the-Horseshoe-Lightship. Led by *Connecticut,* Evans' battle fleet passed in review, maintaining 400 yard intervals, in a single line column that stretched three miles. Sailors, Marines and officers in dress whites and blues manned every deck. Another 21-gun salute boomed out across Chesapeake Bay.

The original plan called for *Mayflower* to sail on to Washington D.C. But an excited commander-in-chief ordered the yacht's captain to follow the fleet. The presidential yacht accompanied the fleet past the Virginia Capes. Once out into the open sea, *Mayflower* hauled up abreast *Connecticut*. And with a final farewell, the president sent his magnificent Great White Fleet with its sixteen first-line battleships crewed by some 14,500 officers and men on its way. The epic journey led by battleship *Connecticut* had begun.

The task force steamed south past Cape Hatteras, bound for the Caribbean. Rear Admiral Evans redeployed his fleet into two squadrons. Each squadron consisted of two divisions, each division a four-ship column. The columns steamed parallel to one another at 1,600 yards apart. Ships maintained intervals of 400 yards in each column.

Rear Admiral Robley D. Evans was not only task force commander, but also commander of First Battleship Squadron as well as First Battleship Division. Proudly flying Evans' flag, *Connecticut* led First Division, followed by *Kansas, Vermont* and *Louisiana.* Rear Admiral William H. Emory commanded Second Division, flying his flag aboard *Georgia,* and was trailed by *New Jersey, Rhode Island* and *Virginia*. Second Battleship Squadron was commanded by Rear Admiral Charles M. Thomas, who in turn commanded Third Division. Thomas flew his flag aboard USS *Minnesota*, ahead of *Ohio, Missouri* and *Maine*. Rear Admiral Charles S. Sperry commanded Fourth Division, flying his flag aboard *Alabama*. In his wake lumbered *Illinois, Kearsarge* and *Kentucky*.

Admiral Evans flashed a signal to his entire command: "The president authorized the Commander-in-Chief to inform the officers and men that after a short stay on the Pacific Coast, it is the president's intention to have the fleet return to the Atlantic Coast by way of the Mediterranean."

On December 20, the fleet approached Puerto Rico. *Kentucky* and *Illinois* dropped out of formation due to engineering problems. However, both ships rejoined the fleet the next day in the Virgin Passage. That same day, a sailor aboard *Alabama* who had died of pneumonia and spinal meningitis was committed to the deep in the Caribbean Sea. Two days later, the fleet closed on Venezuela.

In mid-afternoon, one of the lookouts spotted a white lighthouse. They had reached the Gulf of Paria. The task force twisted and turned its way through the Dragon's Mouth, the treacherous gateway to the Gulf. All the battle-wagons made it through without incident. They steamed in single file towards Port-of-Spain. As the fleet approached the city, it conducted an elaborate maneuver. On signal from *Connecticut*, First Division swung ninety degrees. In turn, each division, on cue, repeated the right angle maneuver with exquisite precision. It was, Admiral Evans later observed, "the finest naval sight ever witnessed."

The fleet was met by a torpedo-boat flotilla which had sailed from Hampton Roads two weeks before. On hand, too, were five colliers loaded with coal. With thirty-two American vessels anchored in the harbor, Port-of-Spain resembled a U.S. Navy base.

The following morning, Admiral Evans and an entourage of officers went ashore to pay their respects to the British Governor-General, Sir Henry Moore Jackson. By now Evans was suffering from rheumatic gout and had to be assisted into one of the waiting carriages by two aides. The Americans were received by Jackson at the Queens Park Hotel.

The fleet spent Christmas in Trinidad. Not all five days were spent in holiday good cheer, as the crews engaged in the backbreaking job of coaling. With all bunkers filled to capacity, the fleet departed Trinidad on December 29, for the 3,400 mile run to Rio de Janiero.

Early in the morning of January 12, 1908, the American fleet was sighted off Cape Frio. Three Brazilian cruisers met the task force twelve miles outside Rio. One of them, *Bar-*

roso, loosed a fifteen-gun salute to Admiral Evans' flag, and then with her sisters, fell into the American formation.

Fort Villagagnon guarded the southern entrance to the harbor. *Connecticut* fired a twenty-one gun salute as it steamed past. Thousands of wildly cheering Brazilians lined the shore to welcome the fleet to Rio. A rigorous schedule of ceremonies, games and festivities ensued, involving everyone from Admiral Evans (now seriously ill) down to the lowliest rating. All were designed to make the Americans feel at home. Government efforts at goodwill extended from President Penna's banquet at the Petropolis to the cooperation extended to the fleet by Vice Admiral Maurity, commander-in-chief of the Brazilian Navy. So successful was the American visit that even the mass waterfront barroom brawl that broke out the first night did nothing to spoil the ten-day visit. Indeed the Great White Fleet's stopover proved a boon to U.S.-Brazilian relations.

On January 22, President Penna bid God-speed to the departing American fleet. Thousands lined the shore to offer their goodwill, braving a downpour until the task force, with its Brazilian naval escort, disappeared from view.

For the next four days, *Connecticut* led the squadron south along the South American continent. At 2000 hours on January 26, the searchlights of the Great White Fleet lit up the heavens. They served as a beacon for the San Martin

Division of the Argentine Navy. Admiral Hopolito Oliva's four cruisers steamed over three hundred miles to meet the American task force. The next morning, the Argentine cruisers *San Martin, Buenos Ayres,* 9 *De Julio* and *Pueyrredon* exchanged gun salutes with the American ships, and the squadrons raised each other's national flags.

Oliva's cruisers departed, leaving the fleet to continue its journey south. Next stop was Chile. At the Straits of Magellan, the fleet deployed into a single column. *Connecticut* led the way into the treacherous waterway that separates mainland Chile from Tierra del Fuego. On February 1, midway through the straits, the fleet dropped anchor at Punta Arenas.

Punta Arenas was a coaling stop. In between replenishing the bunkers of their ships, officers and ratings took advantage of what little diversions there were in the hardscraBBle little town of 14,000 people. On February 6, the fleet left Punta Arenas.

The American ships snaked their way out of the Strait of Magellan and into the Pacific. They headed north and traced the Chilean coast. On February 14, the fleet arrived at Valparaiso. A quarter million people lined the shore. On a hillside overlooking the sea, 500 Chilean sailors, clad in dress whites, spelled WELCOME. The greeting was clearly visible from at least two miles. The training ship *General Baquedano* lay at anchor in the harbor. Aboard were President

Pedro Montt and a host of military and government officials and foreign dignitaries waiting to review the fleet. Led by *Connecticut,* the sixteen battlewagons passed in review of President Montt and answered the cheering throng ashore with a series of thunderous volleys.

The fleet continued north. Five days out of Valparaiso, the Peruvian cruiser *Bolognesi* intercepted the fleet. The *Bolognesi* escorted the task force into Callao Bay on February 20.

The Americans entered Callao Bay to tens of thousands of cheering Peruvians. Evans' fleet entered the bay in squadrons. Upon command, the battlewagons redeployed smartly into divisions. The finely timed maneuver prompted a fifteen-gun salute from Peruvian naval vessels in the harbor. Throwing caution to the wind, thousands of enthusiastic Peruvians descended on the American fleet in an overwhelming force of sailing craft, fishing boats and even row boats.

Because of Admiral Evans' steadily worsening condition, Peruvian President Jose Pardo came aboard *Connecticut* to pay his respects on February 22. A round of social activities followed, including a gala reception held on board *Connecticut* for President Pardo and other Peruvian dignitaries. American sailors were treated to the sights of Lima, including Francisco Pizarro's glass-entombed remains. Under the expressed orders of President Pardo, 3,600 officers and bluejackets were invited to the bull fights. Many Americans found the spectacle disgusting. Some even openly rooted for the animals.

The battleships took on coal from colliers. And on February 29, the fleet was ready for sea. The Peruvian cruiser, *Almirante Grau,* which was flying the flag of President Pardo, steamed by the American battle line. The fleet boomed out a 21-gun salute to Peru. Then in single file, the fleet passed in review of the *Almirante Grau* and exited Callao Bay.

The fleet headed north for Mexico. It arrived at Magdalena Bay on March 20. Here the task force spent the next three weeks engaged in target practice. Colliers rendezvoused with the fleet with fresh coal for empty bunkers. And after a thorough cleaning and a fresh coat of paint, the fleet embarked Magdalena Bay on April 11.

It was during the fleet's hiatus at Magdalena Bay that Admiral Evans, now completely bedridden and in constant pain, was relieved of command. On March 30, *Connecticut* fired up all boilers and barreled north for California. Two days later, BB-18 rendezvoused with USS *Yankton.* Admiral Evans was transferred from his flagship to the tender. He was rushed to a hospital in Paso Robles.

Connecticut hurried south to rejoin the fleet at Magdalena Bay. Here Rear Admiral Charles M. Thomas transferred his flag from *Minnesota.* Thomas was now interim task force commander as the fleet left Mexican waters for California.

The fleet arrived at San Diego on April 14. Four days later, it was in Los Angeles. Here the fleet dispersed into divisions to call on a number of ports including San Pedro, Redondo, Santa Monica, Long Beach, Santa Barbara, Santa Cruz and Monterey. It was in Monterey that Admiral Evans, who had traveled by train the previous night from Paso Robles, was piped aboard the flagship early in the morning of May 5. He was determined to let nothing stand in his way from being on the bridge of *Connecticut* when the fleet made its triumphal entry into San Francisco.

The planners of the round-the-world cruise considered San Francisco the feature port-of-call for the Great White Fleet on its visit to the West Coast. And the city did not disappoint. Over one million people flocked to San Francisco Bay to greet "Fightin' Bob Evans" and the Great White Fleet. The battleships were joined by units of the Pacific Fleet and a torpedo-boat flotilla. There were forty-two warships in all, steaming in a circle two miles wide. It was the most powerful concentration of naval might yet gathered in the Western Hemisphere.

The fleet anchored off the coast. The following morning, May 6, the fleet steamed through the Golden Gate. Up on Telegraph Hill, bright white letters standing fifty feet high spelled "WELCOME." Gun salutes boomed out of the army forts guarding the bay. Secretary of the Navy Metcalf awaited the fleet aboard the gunboat *Yorktown. Connecticut,* leading the procession, fired a seventeen-gun salute to the secretary's flag.

The next day saw a massive parade through the streets of San Francisco. Seven thousand five hundred sailors and Marines, the largest U.S. naval force of men ever landed in peace or war up to that time, were joined by Army regulars, California National Guardsmen, State Police, veterans groups and a host of organizations too numerous to mention. The mayor of San Francisco shared a carriage with Admiral Evans, who braved great pain to acknowledge the cheering multitude that lined the parade route.

On May 8, Secretary Metcalf boarded *Yorktown.* The gunboat sailed up and down the columns of warships anchored in San Francisco Bay, reviewing first the armored cruisers of the Pacific Fleet, then the battleships of the Great White Fleet, First Squadron, and Second Squadron; and last but not least, the lightweights of the fleet, the torpedo-boat flotilla. Each man-of-war had bluejackets and Marines on parade in dress whites and blues, with flags flying and bands blaring.

That evening a gala reception was held at the St. Francis Hotel. It was as much a testimonial for Admiral Evans as it was a celebration for the fleet. Following his farewell address, the stricken fleet commander was assisted to his room upstairs. The next day, "Fightin' Bob Evans" and his family were on a train bound for Washington D.C. and retirement. His naval career, which stretched as far back as the Civil War, was over. The next day, Rear Admiral Charles M. Thomas was named commander of the Great White Fleet.

Admiral Thomas' stint as commander-in-chief was short lived, just six days. He was due for retirement in October, just five months away. And besides, he was afflicted with a heart condition. On May 15, 1908, Rear Admiral Charles Stillman Sperry was named third and final commander of the Great White Fleet.

On May 18, *Connecticut* led the battle fleet north to Puget Sound. People flocked to Seattle, nearly half a million of them from Washington, Oregon, Idaho, Montana and even British Columbia. The stopover was a brief one. First and Third Divisions returned to San Francisco. Second Division visited Bremerton via Tacoma, while Fourth Division sailed straight on to Tacoma. Meanwhile, *Connecticut* entered Hunter's Point Navy Yard for a much needed refit. She was followed in turn by her sisters, as the Great White Fleet was readied for the next leg of the round-the-world cruise.

Two ships were replaced—*Maine* and *Alabama;* the former due to a voracious appetite for coal, and the latter due to a cracked cylinder head. Their replacements were *Nebraska,* fresh from her shakedown cruise, and *Wisconsin,* fresh from a refit.

At 1400 hours, July 7, 1908, *Connecticut* led the Great

White Fleet out of San Francisco Bay. No embarkation ceremonies had been planned. Nevertheless thousands lined the shore to see the fleet off. One ship was missing, *Nebraska*. She had incurred an outbreak of scarlet fever and had to be quarantined. However, local authorities cleared the battlewagon to sail and, after fumigation, departed San Francisco on July 9. She overhauled her sisters five days later. By that time, Admiral Sperry's task force was only 48 hours out of its next port-of-call, Hawaii.

On the morning of July 16, the Hawaiian Islands lay off *Connecticut's* port beam. Admiral Sperry ordered a detour to pass by the island of Malokai. He positioned his fleet so that it was in full view of the island's leper colony. The sufferers streamed out of their houses, waving and cheering the lumbering battlewagons some four miles offshore. Brother Joseph Dutton would later write to Admiral Sperry, "Those sixteen battleships that have the full confidence of America came down the lane with a friendly nod and passed on, so dignified and beautiful, this early July morning … It makes us better Americans and may God bless everyone who has even a little to do with bringing about this great pleasure. In all this I am speaking for the people of the leper settlement."

Following this gesture of goodwill, Sperry ordered Third Division to Lahaina for coaling. The balance of the fleet steamed for Diamond Head. Thousands lined the coast and beaches. Countless yachts and boats, many colorfully decorated, greeted the fleet. Due to the narrow confines of Honolulu Harbor, only *Connecticut* and First Division entered. The remainder of the fleet anchored outside. A system of relay was implemented whereby ships entered the harbor singly to coal.

That afternoon, the Governor of Hawaii came aboard *Connecticut* to acknowledge Admiral Sperry. The following day saw a round of diplomatic visits to BB-18 by dignitaries from England, Mexico, Peru, Germany, Sweden, Norway, Portugal, Japan, China and France. Ashore, officers, bluejackets and Marines were treated like royalty for the next five days between luaus, parades and the beaches. On July 18, there occurred an engineering mishap aboard *Kearsarge*. A steam pipe ruptured, injuring five crewmen. Damage was minimal, and the steam plant was repaired in less than half a day. The fleet's scheduled embarkation was not delayed. And on July 22, Sperry's task force put to sea.

The next stop was Auckland, New Zealand. This was the longest leg of the journey at 3,850 miles. Such a distance was not a problem for such long-legged ships like *Connecticut* and *Virginia*. But short-legged ships like *Illinois* and *Wisconsin* could find the Auckland run a challenge to their endurance. And no one in the fleet wanted to endure the embarrassment of having his ship towed into port. Tight control was maintained over coal supplies. Mistakes made in fuel efficiency while rounding South America earlier in the voyage were corrected. The engineering crews developed and honed their skills, which allowed their ships to operate in the vaster stretches of the Pacific with an efficiency not thought possible. Indeed the United States Navy gained priceless experience in the area of long-range cruise control because of the Great White Fleet.

Twenty-four hours out of Auckland, the squadron was buffeted by high winds and heavy seas. But the task force weathered the storm in fine shape and arrived on schedule on August 9.

At 0710 hours, the New Zealand maritime training ship, NZS *Amokura,* fired a thirteen-gun salute to the approaching squadron. Some hundred thousand spectators lined Waitemata Harbor and Rangitoto Channel. Sixteen gleaming white battleships appeared out of the morning mist. *Connecticut* led the procession through an S-shaped maneuver that sent the New Zealanders cheering. Then, under escort by a fleet of local boats, the American ships sailed into Waitemata Harbor and there dropped anchor. For the next five days, Americans and New Zealanders mingled in a camaraderie based on common language and heritage. Special races were held at Ellerslie Racetrack. Sailors and Marines were shown the sights, such as the Rotorua Thermal Springs.

Members of parliament and their families were piped aboard *Connecticut* on August 11 for a gala. On August 14, Governor Lord Plunkett reviewed the fleet. The task force departed Auckland the next day. Prime Minister Sir Joseph Ward, on board a government steamer, acknowledged the fleet as it passed in review. *Connecticut* led the procession as Ward saluted each ship in turn. On each quarter deck, the battleship's band played the national anthem of both nations. As the final ship in line, *Kentucky,* steamed by, Prime Minister Ward led his entourage in three rousing cheers for the United States.

The Great White Fleet skirted New Zealand's North Cape and filtered into the Tasman Sea and ran smack into the teeth of an angry gale. For two days, the battleships tossed about the heavy, pitching seas. On the evening of August 19, the weather relented. The fleet emerged intact and pushed on to Australia over placid seas.

Ashore, the anticipation was electric. More than half a million people were already camped out, from Manly to North Head and from Botany Bay to South Head. At 0500, August 20, mastheads poked up from the horizon. One by one, silhouettes took shape until suddenly sixteen battleships lumbered into view and closed the coast in single-line formation.

By 9:00 a.m., the fleet was off Botany Bay and completely ringed in by countless numbers of small craft. Inside the circle, Admiral Sperry maneuvered his ships into a huge square and made for Sydney Harbor. *Connecticut* passed North Head and fired a twenty-one gun salute to Fort Denison. The garrison inside the fort replied in kind. The task force broke into divisions. Each ship in turn was directed to a prearranged anchorage. All along the shore, bands and orchestras played the Star Spangled Banner and other American patriotic songs

The Australians had planned for this visit for a long time, and Sydney had no intention of being outdone by any other city. A plethora of activities had been planned—banquets and balls, galas and games, teas and tours. Americans and Australians competed against one another in such sports as boomerang throwing, buck jumping, wood chopping, rifle matches, boxing and baseball.

The highlight of the fleet's visit occurred on August 23. The site was Centennial Park. Twelve thousand men of the United States Navy, Royal Navy and Commonwealth naval and military forces of New South Wales paraded before a quarter million cheering people. It was one of the most memorable events in the history of Sydney.

Three more days of celebration came to an end on August 27, when the fleet got up steam and weighed anchor. Tens of thousands saw the fleet off. Many a bluejacket and Marine would never forget the hospitality of this great city.

Likewise, they would never forget the cordiality of their next port-of-call. Two nights and six hundred miles later, the task force was outside Melbourne.

1100 hours, August 29, the fleet skirted Port Philip Head for the thirty mile run to Hobson's Bay. Just like at Sydney, the task force became besieged by a fleet of steamers and small craft.

The battleships anchored in Hobson's Bay around 1500 hours. The next day, Sunday, 1,000 sailors attended a pontifical mass at St. Patrick's Cathedral. On Monday, the official festivities to welcome the fleet began with banquets, games and theater performances. At the end of the day, the Americans joined in on a huge torchlight procession through the city.

Thursday was proclaimed a holiday in Melbourne. Crowds gathered for the planned military review. But the stars on this occasion were not the American sailors, but the naval cadets of Ballarat. These young lads, ages 11 to 16, eschewed public transportation and marched eighty miles in five days. These sailors in the making captured the hearts and minds of the American bluejackets. Many were actually carried along the parade route by jubilant Yanks.

Many American sailors enjoyed much free time while in Melbourne. It was not uncommon to see a Yank with a girl on each arm. In fact, a dinner set for three thousand American sailors drew a grand total of seven. Such was the time the visitors were having on the streets.

The finale of the Melbourne visit was a massive fireworks display at Albert Park. This wonderful city down under was viewed overwhelmingly by American sailors as the favored liberty port for the entire cruise. And apparently such was the case, as 221 bluejackets were AWOL for Saturday morning muster. The following day, September 6, *Connecticut* slipped her moorings and led the fleet, save *Kansas*, out to sea. *Kansas* was detached to collect the mail and round up as many stragglers as could be found.

Connecticut led the task force across the Great Australian Bight, a body of water renown for its huge swells. Yet despite the heavy seas, the 1,300 mile transit proved largely uneventful. And on September 11, the fleet arrived at Albany.

Albany is on the southwestern tip of Australia. Though a small city, it proved just as hospitable a community as either Sydney or Melbourne. However, the main reason for the stopover was to coal and provision each ship for the 3,500 mile hike to Manila.

On September 15, *Kansas* rejoined the fleet with 458 bags of mail and over one hundred strays. That left more than one hundred deserters still at large. However, with a schedule to keep, these men were written off. And on September 19, the Great White Fleet was again pounding the seas.

The task force rounded the west coast of Australia and steamed north through the Indian Ocean. By the 26th, the fleet was off Bali. It cut through the Lombok Strait, broke into the Java Sea, then cut north toward Borneo. With her sisters in van, *Connecticut* sliced through the Makassar Strait, pushed into the Celebes Sea and closed on Mindanao.

Connecticut led a single-line column through the Basilan Strait towards Zamboanga. As the battleships passed the largest city on Mindanao, they loosed a twenty-one gun salute.

Three days later, on October 2, *Connecticut* led her charges past Corregidor and into Manila Bay. The Philippine capital was caught in the throes of a cholera epidemic. Planned festivities ashore were canceled. For the next eight days, crews were confined to their ships. They were kept busy coaling and refitting their ships for the next leg of the journey. On October 10, 1908, the fleet departed Manila Bay for Yokohama.

Connecticut and her consorts steamed north through the South China Sea. The weather was calm and the sea was like glass, a mariner's cause for concern. Barometers plummeted. Skies darkened. Seas rose, then became tumultuous. By the morning of October 12, the squadron was in the grips of a typhoon. Ships became scattered. Some cut their engines and rode the rollers. Ships with low freeboard suffered most. Aboard *Missouri,* those on watch on the bridge were continually drenched with waves and spray. Atop *Kearsarge*, the foretopmast and radio antenna were ripped from their moorings and tossed in the sea. *Rhode Island*, bringing up the rear, lost three men washed overboard. Two were plucked from the raging seas. But the third was swept away in full view of his would be rescuers.

The seas relented. The skies cleared. In two days it was over. Scattered units were gathered, and damage was repaired. Signals sent informed Tokyo of a twenty-four hour delay in the fleet's arrival. The rest of the voyage through the North Pacific proved uneventful.

On October 18, *Connecticut*, at the head of First Division, closed Yokohama. Her wireless operator became bombarded with signals of welcome from Japanese civil and military authorities. Three Japanese men-of-war and six merchantmen joined up as escort. The black hulls of the merchantmen were emblazoned with WELCOME in large white letters. Aboard, men, women and children cheered and sang American patriotic songs.

The heavy mist that enshrouded the fleet's approach dissipated as the ships entered Tokyo. American battleships, white and gleaming, exchanged volleys of salute with the gray and drab but efficient-looking Japanese men-of-war.

The Japanese were well aware of the efforts made by the Australians and New Zealanders to make the Americans feel at home and had no desire to come out second best. Tokyo had planned an impressive array of festivities. On the visitor's side, sensitivity to the host's mores of politeness and courtesy was vigorously pursued.

Admiral Sperry went ashore and attended a garden party given by the city officials of Yokohama. The officers and men of BB-18 and her sister ships were paraded through the streets of Tokyo, past cheering crowds waving American and Japanese flags. Their triumph concluded at the village of Uraga, where Commodore Perry landed more than fifty years before.

October 19 was proclaimed American Day in Tokyo. Over 1,000 school children welcomed Admiral Sperry to the city. Later the fleet commander and his officers were entertained in the garden of the empress. All the flag officers and their aides were housed in the Shiba Detached Palace. Battleship skippers were lodged at the Imperial Hotel. All were guests of the emperor until October 23. In fact, the emperor himself attended a luncheon for his guests on the 20th.

On the 23rd, flag officers and ship commanders were feted to a dinner aboard the battleship *Fuji*. This was followed up by a reception aboard the battleship *Mikasa*. The next day, Japanese naval officers were honored with a dinner and reception aboard *Connecticut*.

October 25 was the day of departure. An entourage of

Japanese officials, led by the vice minister of foreign affairs, was accorded full honors aboard *Connecticut.* The ceremony was brief. After the Japanese dignitaries had departed, *Connecticut* and her sisters got up steam. BB-18, taking her rightful place as flagship, preceded the task force into the inner harbor. Once there each ship executed a tight turn and headed for the open sea. The Japanese cruisers *Kashima, Isukuha,* and *Katori* tagged along as escort. And as the Americans departed, the Japanese warships rendered volleys of salute.

Twenty-four hours out of Japan, Second Squadron peeled off and steamed for Amoy. *Connecticut* and First Squadron pressed on towards the Philippines, arriving at Subic Bay on the morning of October 31, 1908. Second Squadron departed Amoy on November 5 to rejoin First Squadron at Subic. Here the fleet engaged in range calibration exercises, then headed for Manila Bay and battle practice. For the next three weeks, the crews busied themselves with coaling and provisioning the ships and taking part in festivities and celebrations ashore. On December 1, the fleet departed Manila Bay.

The Great White Fleet crossed the South China Sea for Singapore. On December 6, as the fleet neared the British possession, *Connecticut* boomed out a twenty-one gun salute to the delight of those in the boats and ships that had gathered to review the squadron's sail-by.

The fleet steamed up the Strait of Malacca. Two days up the waterway that separates Sumatra from Malaya, *New Jersey* signaled men overboard. All ships stopped. Boats were lowered and searchlights probed the darkness. Only one man was plucked from the black waters. *New Jersey* was detached to continue the search for its missing crewman while the rest of the fleet pushed on. Sailors from the *New Jersey* continued the search for several hours, but the canvas proved fruitless, and they were recalled. The battleship sped out of the Malacca Strait and rejoined the fleet in the Andaman Sea.

The weather in the Bay of Bengal was better than hoped for, and the task force arrived at Ceylon (Sri Lanka) on December 12, one day ahead of schedule. Early the following morning, *Connecticut* led the fleet round Point de Galle and into Colombo.

Colombo was a planned coal stop. The battleships simply lacked the bunker capacity for a non-stop run from Manila Bay to the Suez Canal. While in port, the crews pursued official and unofficial activities, which provided a respite from the drudgeries of coaling and provisioning their ships. On December 20, *Connecticut* led the Great White Fleet out of Colombo and into the Arabian Sea.

The weather was placid and the seas were calm, just the conditions for drills. Every day crews engaged in maneuvers, battle drills, signal drills, range-finding drills and searchlight drills. Aboard *Connecticut,* to relieve the tension, the orchestra assembled every evening on the quarter deck and played from 8:00 p.m. to 9:00 p.m.

The day after Christmas, the island of Socotra was sighted. The task force pushed into the Gulf of Aden, rounded Yemen and broke into the Red Sea. As the battleships steamed north, they passed heavy traffic streaming south. One such was a British troopship bound for India. Tommies gathered on deck and offered the American squadron three rousing cheers. On January 3, 1909, the Great White Fleet reached the southern gateway to the Suez Canal and there, dropped anchor. It was two days ahead of schedule.

The Great White Fleet posed the largest single group of ships to ever traverse the Suez Canal up to that time. The entire canal was closed to all other traffic to accommodate Sperry's task force. Flagship *Connecticut* entered first, followed in turn by her sisters. It took three days to process all sixteen battleships through the Canal; after which they made for Port Said.

The Egyptian port was a coaling stop. When all bunkers were replenished, the fleet dispersed to call on various ports throughout the Mediterranean. First Division would visit Italy, then on to Villefranche on the French Riviera. Second Division was ordered to Marseilles. Third Division would assume two groups and visit Greek and Turkish ports, while Fourth Division would put into Malta, Tripoli and Algiers.

Southern Italy had been wracked by an earthquake. Admiral Sperry ordered *Connecticut* and *Illinois* to proceed with all possible speed to Messina to render assistance. Seamen from *Connecticut* pitched in to clear ruBBle, distribute food to hard-pressed survivors and unload relief supplies from the transport USS *Culgoa*. A detachment of petty officers from BB-18 acted as a guard of honor at the funeral of the British Consul's wife. King Victor Emmanuel granted an audience to Admiral Sperry and personally thanked the fleet commander for the valuable assistance.

The end of January saw the Great White Fleet assemble in Gibraltar for the final leg of the voyage. *Connecticut* arrived with First Division. The Royal Navy battleships *Albemarle* and *Albion,* the Second Cruiser Squadron, the Russian battleships *Tsarevitch* and *Slava,* cruisers *Bogatyr* and *Oleg,* and French and Dutch gunboats received them. All with decks manned and bands blaring. *Connecticut* fired a volley in salute, a gesture returned by *Albemarle* and batteries ashore.

The fleet spent the next five days coaling, some 1,500 tons per vessel. Those crew members not engaged in this dirty job took part in games, festivities and sports with their British counterparts. Especially popular were the rowing competitions and boxing. By Saturday, February 6, 1909, Sperry's task force was ready for sea.

At 0900 hours, the Great White Fleet got up steam under a bright sun and clear skies. British bands belted out "Auld Lang Syne" and "For He's a Jolly Good Fellow" as Yankee ships passed by. In ninety minutes, fifteen battleships cleared the harbor and formed a straight-line formation to await the flagship. *Connecticut* began to edge out of the harbor. Vice Admiral Goodrich, RN, ordered his flagship HMS *Devonshire* to fire a twenty-one gun salute. In return, Admiral Sperry ordered *Connecticut's* band to strike up "God Save the King." *Devonshire's* musicians replied with the "Star Spangled Banner."

Connecticut cleared the harbor. She steamed along the gleaming white line of warships waiting for her. She assumed her position as lead ship and shaped a course for the Atlantic. The fleet was going home.

Admiral Sperry intended to put his squadron through extensive drills and exercises. This was to be followed by each ship undergoing the annual admiral's inspection. But the Atlantic refused to cooperate. And for three days, the fleet endured high winds and heavy seas.

The weather subsided and the drills began. There were daytime exercises and nighttime exercises. But on February

14, the high winds and heavy seas returned, and the drills were curtailed.

Meanwhile stateside preparations for the fleet's arrival proceeded apace. Included was Rear Admiral Conway H. Arnold's task force, which featured battleships *Maine, Idaho, Mississippi* and *New Hampshire*, two armored and three scout cruisers. This force departed Hampton Roads on February 14. Three days later, the two task forces linked up. Now more than two dozen warships would make the triumphal entry into Hampton Roads.

1100 hours, February 22, 1909—George Washington's birthday—*Connecticut* led twenty-six men-of-war round Tail-of-the-Horseshoe-Lightship. Each ship, ensigns and pennants flying proudly, passed in review of President Theodore Roosevelt aboard *Mayflower*. A moved president acknowledged each twenty-one gun salute. When the last warship had passed in review, *Mayflower* fell astern the seven mile long column.

Connecticut preceded her sisters into the Roads past the wildly cheering crowds ashore. Somewhere a band broke into "There's No Place Like Home." BB-18 resumed her anchorage off Old Point Comfort. The venerable battle-wagon had led the intrepid fleet from start to finish. Flag officers may have changed, but flagships had not. President Roosevelt was piped aboard. In a short address he said to her crew, "You've done the trick. Other nations may do as you have done, but they'll have to follow you."

With that, the cruise was officially over. So ended one of the greatest feats in modern maritime history, that of circumnavigation of the globe by sixteen coal-burning battleships. USS *Connecticut,* flagship of the Great White Fleet, had secured a storied place in American naval annals. In so doing, BB-18 had steamed an astounding 46,729 miles.

PREWAR SERVICE

On March 8, 1909, Rear Admiral Charles S. Sperry relinquished *Connecticut* as his flagship to Rear Admiral Seaton Schroeder. Admiral Schroeder retained *Connecticut* as flagship of the Atlantic Fleet. That afternoon, *Connecticut* cleared Hampton Roads for the New York Navy Yard. Following an overhaul, BB-18 called on Boston. After a short stay, *Connecticut* participated in maneuvers off Provincetown; then it was on to the Virginia Capes. On September 21, she was back in New York. *Connecticut* was to be the host vessel for the Hudson-Fulton Celebration.

Rear Admiral Schroeder participated in the official reception ashore on September 25. That evening, he played host as commander-in-chief to an elaborate dinner aboard his flagship to a number of ship captains and divisional officers from Argentina, France, Germany, Great Britain and Italy. On September 30, Marines and four companies of sailors from *Connecticut* took part in festivities held at Columbia University. *Connecticut* concluded its participation in the Hudson-Fulton Celebration with a cruise up the Hudson River on October 9.

Connecticut spent the next couple of months on duty at Hampton Roads and Tompkinsville before returning to New York. Then on January 7, 1910, BB-18 upped anchor and steamed for Guantanamo Bay. She remained in Cuban waters for two months conducting maneuvers and battle practice.

On March 28, *Connecticut* sailed north for the States. Following a short stay at Hampton Roads, she headed for New York and another refit. It was while in New York that on May 19, Ensign Raymond Spruance reported for duty. This was the beginning of an illustrious career that was to take the young ensign to the surrender ceremonies in Tokyo Bay thirty-five years later as Commander-in-Chief United States Fifth Fleet.

Following her overhaul, *Connecticut* sailed north for New England waters and spent several months on maneuvers and battle practice.

USS *Connecticut* returned to New York. On November 2, she embarked for Europe on a midshipman cruise. BB-18 arrived at Portland, England on November 15. *Connecti-*

cut, as flagship of the U.S. Atlantic Fleet, received Admiral William H. May, Commander-in-Chief Home Fleet Royal Navy. Accompanying the British fleet commander was Vice Admiral Callaghan, commander of the British Second Battle Squadron, flying his flag aboard HMS *King Edward V*II, and Rear Admiral Sir Charles J. Colville, commander of the First Cruiser Squadron.

On December 1, in honor of Queen Mother Alexandra's birthday, *Connecticut,* fully dressed and flying a British Ensign, fired her main armament in salute. Many of her crew were granted shore leave to attend a huge dinner and dance in Portland.

Connecticut departed Portland for Cherbourg, France, arriving on December 8. Two days later, the commander-in-chief of the French Navy was piped aboard. Over the next several weeks, many of *Connecticut's* midshipmen and crew enjoyed shore leave. On Christmas Day, a boat race was staged. A race boat from *Connecticut* squared off against a challenger from the French man-of-war *Charles Martel.* The Yanks beat the French handily by twelve lengths.

On December 28, Rear Admiral Schroeder hosted a reception on board *Connecticut* for officers of the French Navy and residents of Cherbourg. Two days later, *Connecticut* departed France for winter operations in Guantanamo Bay.

On March 17, 1911, *Connecticut* returned to Hampton

Roads and took part in maneuvers off the U.S. coast, exercises that took her as far north as Provincetown, Massachusetts.

On June 1, 1911, Rear Admiral Schroeder lowered his flag in lieu of that of Rear Admiral Hugo Osterhaus, who had been captain of the *Connecticut* during the round-the-world cruise.

On November 2, USS *Connecticut* led the Presidential Review of the Fleet in New York. She maintained station in New York waters until January 12, 1912, when she sailed for Guantanamo Bay to take part in winter exercises. She returned to Hampton Roads on March 21, and from there, entered the Philadelphia Navy Yard for an overhaul on April 12. While *Connecticut* was dockside, Rear Admiral Osterhaus transferred his flag to battleship *Washington*. His flag secretary at the time happened to be none other than Ernest J. King, who would later become Commander-in-Chief United States Navy during World War II.

Following her refit, USS *Connecticut* spent the rest of 1912 engaged in torpedo practice at Fort Pond Bay, then in fleet maneuvers and battle practice off Block Island and the Virginia Capes. At the conclusion of this duty, *Connecticut* returned to New York for dockyard service in preparation for winter exercises. Meanwhile Rear Admiral Osterhaus was relieved as Commander-in-Chief Atlantic Fleet and replaced by Rear Admiral Charles J. Badger. Admiral Badger flew his flag aboard *Wyoming*, newly commissioned to the fleet.

USS *Connecticut* departed New York Harbor on February 13, 1913 for Guantanamo Bay. Here she engaged in maneuvers and training. On the 28th, *Connecticut* again assumed the role of Flagship Atlantic Fleet. The duty was short-lived, as Admiral Badger transferred his flag to battleship *Utah*. On March 20, *Connecticut* sped first to Hampton Roads and then to Philadelphia. Here she took on stores and then shaped a course for Mexico. She arrived off Tampico on April 22. For the next two months, BB-18 patrolled the waters off Tampico and Vera Cruz in the protection of American lives and property.

Connecticut departed Tampico on June 22. The next three months saw the battleship in dry dock in the Philadelphia Navy Yard, followed by gunnery practice off the Virginia Capes. She was back at Hampton Roads in October. On the 23rd, Rear Admiral Frank E. Beatty broke out his flag. *Connecticut* was now Flagship Fourth Battleship Division, Atlantic Fleet.

On October 25, 1913, *Connecticut* led Fourth Division in review before the Secretary of the Navy. Immediately following this formality, the battleship put to sea. Destination was Genoa, Italy. *Connecticut* remained in Italian waters, showing the flag until November 30, when she was ordered to Vera Cruz. *Connecticut* arrived in Mexican waters on December 23. Three days later, Rear Admiral Henry T. Mayo came aboard to assume command of Fourth Battleship Division. The outgoing Rear Admiral Beatty assumed command of First Battleship Division.

Connecticut spent the next several months on a shuttle run between Vera Cruz and Tampico, lifting refugees out of harm's way. She departed Mexico in April and arrived at Galveston, Texas, on the 26th, putting ashore 886 refugees. She returned to Tampico on May 5, 1914, shuttling officers of the U.S. Army and representatives of the American Red Cross. That same month, on the 29th, Rear Admiral Mayo transferred his flag to battleship *Minnesota*. *Connecticut* continued peacekeeping duties until July 2, when she departed Vera Cruz for Havana, Cuba. She departed Havana July 8 with the American minister to Haiti on board, arriving at Port-au-Prince on the 13th. *Connecticut* remained in Haiti until August 8, when she departed for Philadelphia. She arrived on August 14, 1914.

THE WAR YEARS

While Europe embroiled itself in the titanic struggle on the continent, America remained neutral. But neutrality did not mean a period of lethargy for the United States Navy. *Con-*

necticut took part in battle practice off the shores of Maine and the Virginia Capes. Then on October 1, *Connecticut* put into the Philadelphia Navy Yard for an overhaul, remaining in the City of Brotherly Love until January 15, 1915.

Connecticut steamed for Cuba, conducting training exercises in CariBBean waters. She returned to Philadelphia, remaining on station until July 31, 1915, when she sailed for Haiti. On board were 433 officers and men of the Second Regiment, First Brigade, United States Marine Corps. The leathernecks were put ashore at Port-au-Prince on August 5.

Connecticut delivered stores and equipment to amphibious troops at Cape Haiten on September 5. BB-18 remained on station in support of the landing parties ashore. One such was a detachment of Marines and sailors from the *Connecticut* under the command of Major Smedley Darlington Butler. This intrepid leatherneck was one of the most colorful Marines in the entire history of the Corps. On April 22, 1914, Butler earned a Medal of Honor for his heroic actions at Vera Cruz. On November 17, 1915, Butler earned a second Medal of Honor for leading his sailors and Marines in an attack on Fort Riviere against forces of the Caco resistance. Butler is only one of two Marines to be awarded the Medal of Honor more than once.

Connecticut returned to Philadelphia on December 15, 1915. Upon arrival, BB-18 was placed in the Atlantic Fleet Reserve.

Unrestricted submarine warfare in the Atlantic by Germany brought America closer to war. On October 3, 1916, USS *Connecticut* returned to active duty. Two days later, Rear Admiral H.O. Dunn transferred his flag from *Minnesota,* as *Connecticut* assumed the role of Flagship Fifth Battleship Division. *Connecticut* took part in maneuvers in Caribbean waters briefly before returning to the United States.

Connecticut was assigned to a variety of training duties on the Atlantic seaboard. Raw sailors from the training station at Portsmouth, Virginia, took part in exercises on her decks off Chesapeake Bay to the Virginia Capes. More than a thousand bluejackets were trained aboard BB-18 as gun crewmen for duty on U.S. merchant ships. Many midshipmen from Annapolis trained for duty overseas on board *Connecticut.* In addition, *Connecticut* served as Flagship Fifth Battleship Division, flying the flags of Rear Admiral T.S. Rodgers and Rear Admiral J.H. Glennon.

Connecticut finished World War I assigned to Second Battleship Squadron, Fourth Battleship Division, Atlantic Fleet.

POSTWAR SERVICE

USS *Connecticut* departed Hampton Roads on January 6, 1919 for Brest, France. She took on more than one thousand American troops and ferried them back to New York, arriving on February 2. On February 25, *Connecticut* departed Hampton Roads, again bound for Brest. She lifted stateside 1,240 men of the Fifty-Third Pioneer Regiment, a company of Marines and a company of Military Police, arriving at Hampton Roads on March 24.

Two months later, *Connecticut* made her third trip to France. Following a short liberty for her crew in Paris, *Connecticut* transported 891 men of the 502ⁿᵈ Army Engineers, a medical detachment and representatives of the American Red Cross. BB-18 disembarked her passengers at Newport News, Virginia, on June 22, 1919. *Connecticut* left Newport News for Philadelphia. Here Vice Admiral Hilary P. Jones, commander of Second Battleship Squadron, hoisted his flag.

Connecticut spent the next eleven months based out of Philadelphia training midshipmen. On May 20, 1920, BB-18 arrived at Annapolis to pick up 200 midshipmen for a training cruise. The next day, *Connecticut* and Second Battleship Squadron put to sea. The task force transited the Panama Canal on the way to Honolulu. Seattle was the next port-of-call, then south to San Francisco and San Pedro. Following the last named port, the task force headed home via the Panama Canal. The canal was three days astern when *Connecticut's* port engine quit. *New Hampshire* took her stricken sister in tow, arriving at Guantanamo Bay on August 28. Vice Admiral Jones transferred his flag to battleship *Kansas*.

The midshipmen were debarked as well, and *Connecticut* was towed stateside by *Promethus*. The pair arrived at the Philadelphia Navy Yard on September 11, 1920.

On March 21, 1921, Rear Admiral Charles F. Hughes broke out his flag. USS *Connecticut* was now Flagship Second Battleship Squadron, Atlantic Fleet. *Connecticut* departed Philadelphia on April 7 to take part in maneuvers and training exercises with her division in Cuban waters. She returned to Hampton Roads in time for the Presidential Review on April 28. On Memorial Day, *Connecticut* joined in on holiday activities at the Naval Academy at Annapolis.

On June 3, *Connecticut* and Second Battleship Squadron embarked on another midshipman cruise. Destination was Christiania, Norway. On June 28, Haakon VII, King of Norway, was piped aboard *Connecticut* for a reception. He was joined by the Prime Minister of Norway, the Norwegian Minister of Defense and the First Sea Lord of the Norwegian Navy, Admiral Bergtund.

The squadron sailed for Portugal, arriving at Lisbon on July 21, 1921. *Connecticut* hosted the Civil Governor of the Province of Lisbon and the Commander-in-Chief of the Portuguese Navy. On July 27, the President of Portugal was piped aboard. He was received by Captain Ralph Earle and the skippers of *Kansas, South Carolina, Michigan* and *Minnesota*.

Two days later, the American ships crossed the Atlantic for Guantanamo Bay. The squadron remained in Cuban waters for the next several weeks engaged in gunnery practice and battle exercises. It was also the end of the midshipman cruise. *Connecticut* left her squadron and sailed for Annapolis, arriving on August 30. She disembarked her midshipmen, and then sailed on to Philadelphia.

On September 17, Rear Admiral Hughes was reassigned to the Pacific Fleet as Commander-in-Chief Battleship Division Seven. *Connecticut,* too, was transferred to the Pacific. She steamed out of Philadelphia for the last time on October 4, 1921, and arrived at San Diego on October 27. Rear Admiral H.O. Stickney, Commander-in-Chief Pacific Fleet Training, broke out his flag. Admiral Stickney retained *Connecticut* until he was relieved by Rear Admiral John V. Chase on December 8. The change of command was short-lived, for *Connecticut* had finished her final posting.

Ever changing naval design and technology had rendered BB-18 obsolete. She had been reduced to the status of a bargaining chip to meet the conditions of the Washington Naval Treaty of February 8, 1922.

USS *Connecticut* got up steam for the last time on December 11, 1922. She left San Pedro and reached Puget Sound Navy Yard five days later. She was decommissioned on March 1, 1923. She was sold for scrap on November 1, 1923 to Mr. Walter W. Johnson of San Francisco for $42,750.

So ended the career of battleship *Connecticut,* and an illustrious career it was. She was the lead ship of a class of battleship that proved the epitome of American pre-dreadnought design. She was flagship of the Atlantic Fleet more than once and flagship of numerous battleship squadrons and divisions. Yet her greatest honor was as flagship of President Theodore Roosevelt's Great White Fleet. The round-the-world cruise was one of the shining moments of the United States Navy. And *Connecticut* led the endeavor from start to finish, leading her squadron through fair seas and foul, playing host to foreign dignitaries and world leaders, showing the flag with such power and grace that she exemplified all the best that America and her navy stand for.

PART THREE

BATTLESHIP FACTS AND TIDBITS

- Throughout the narrative, battleship *Connecticut* is frequently referred to as BB-18. On July 20, 1920, the U.S. Navy instituted the alphanumeric designation "BB" for each and every battleship. Ships authorized prior to July 20 were simply back-numbered. Ships after July 20 carried forward the "BB" designation until the last battleship had been authorized.

- On January 8, 1907, President Theodore Roosevelt signed an Executive Order mandating that the prefix "uss" precede the name of every U.S. Navy vessel. uss means United States Ship.

- Connecticut and her sisters formed the largest single class of battleships completed in U.S. naval history. There were six ships, and they were as follows: uss

Connecticut (BB-18), uss *Louisiana* (BB-19), uss *Vermont* (BB-20), uss *Kansas* (BB-21), uss *Minnesota* (BB-22) and uss *New Hampshire* (BB-25).

- A distinctive hallmark of American battleship design was the cage mast. Known also as the lattice or basket mast, it was introduced in 1908. Despite its fragile appearance, the cage mast was designed to take numerous hits before toppling. It was a design cue that was to last for several decades. In fact, battleships *West Virginia*, *Tennessee*, *Maryland* and *California* still sported their basket masts at the time of the Pearl Harbor attack on December 7, 1941. The *Connecticuts* had their original pole masts removed and their cage masts installed during the class's 1910–11 refit.

- *Connecticut* and her sisters were equipped with coal-fired power plants. Prior to World War I, coal was the fuel of the day. Coal was cheap, and it was plentiful. Oil had been tried as a fuel as far back as 1867. Oil was cleaner, more efficient and easier to handle. But supplies of oil were scarce, and it was cost prohibitive. It was not until 1909 that the U.S. Navy began to make the change to oil-fired power plants. By 1910, all new destroyers and submarines burned oil. Battleships *North Carolina* (BB-29) and *Florida* (BB-30) were the

Navy's first hybrid capital ships, which meant they burned both oil and coal. It was not until uss *Nevada* (BB-36), launched in 1914 that American battleships burned oil exclusively.

• The sixteen battleships sent round the world by President Theodore Roosevelt on December 16, 1907 have been known ever since as the Great White Fleet. In reality, American warships had been painted white since the 1880s. The color made American ships distinctive and easily identifiable. It also made American ships lovely targets, as was realized during the round-the-world cruise. Upon the fleet's return, American men-of-war were painted gray.

• The cruise of the Great White Fleet laid bare certain design flaws which were inherent in American battleship design. One such was armor protection. It was found that the armor belts did not extend low enough down the hull to provide protection against torpedo hits when the ships were in near empty condition. Conversely, when the ships were heavily laden, the armor belts did not extend high enough to provide protection against shellfire. Such design flaws were corrected in later battleship designs.

- Another flaw in *Connecticut's* design were the 12 seven-inch quick fire guns mounted in casemates along the hull. The seven-inch projectile had been viewed by the Navy as the largest round that could be hand loaded and rapidly fired. However, at 165 pounds, the seven-inch round proved too heavy to handle for rapid fire. Later American designs would mount the more manageable five-inch gun. It was also found that the seven-inchers were mounted too low down the hull and therefore were useless in heavy seas. The seven-inchers were removed from the entire *Connecticut* class in 1917, and their casemates were plated over.

- American battleships were named after states. One was not—USS *Kearsarge* (BB-05). *Kearsarge* was so-named by an Act of Congress in commemoration of the Union man-of-war that sank the notorious Confederate raider *Alabama* during the Civil War. It is indeed interesting to note that the only battleship not named after a state would go on to enjoy the longest term of uninterrupted service of any battleship in U.S. Navy history. *Kearsarge* was launched on March 24, 1898 and was commissioned on February 20, 1900. *Kearsarge* served as an active duty battleship for twenty years, until August 5, 1920. She was then converted to a crane ship with the alphanumeric designation AB-1. It was in this capacity that *Kearsarge* raised the sunken submarine *Squalus* from a watery grave in 1939. On November 6, 1941, the name *Kearsarge* was transferred to the aircraft carrier CV-12, then under construction. But AB-1 continued to serve the Navy as a crane ship for another fourteen years. She was struck from the Navy list on June 22, 1955 and sold for scrap on August 9, 1955 after 55 years of continuous service.

Roster of Commanding Officers, Battleship Connecticut.

- Captain William Swift

  September 29, 1906-April 4, 1907

- Captain Hugo Osterhaus

  April 4, 1907-March 21, 1909

- Lieutenant-Commander Louis de Steiguer

  March 21, 1909-April 21, 1909

- Captain John M. Bowyer

  April 21, 1909-June 1, 1909

- Captain Walter C. Cowles

  June 1, 1909-November 1, 1909

- Captain Albert W. Grant

  November 1, 1909-March 9, 1910

- Commander Josiah S. McKean

  March 9, 1910-March 15, 1910

- Captain William R. Rush

  March 15, 1910-January 2, 1912

- Captain Hugh Rodman

  January 2, 1912-October 24, 1912

- Captain John J. Knapp   October 24, 1912-October 24, 1914

- Lieutenant-Commander Ivan C. Wettengel   October 24, 1914-December 28, 1914

- Captain Edward H. Durell   December 28, 1914-October 25, 1916

- Captain Andrew T. Long   October 25, 1916-February 13, 1918

- Commander John S. Abbott   February 13, 1918-February 17, 1918

- Captain James F. Carter   February 17, 1918-April 7, 1919

- Captain Yates Stirling, Jr.   April 7, 1919-April 15, 1920

- Commander Robert E. Ingersol   April 15, 1920-May 5, 1920

- Captain Ralph Earle   May 5, 1920-September 28, 1921

- Captain George L.P. Stone   September 28, 1921-March 1, 1923

The Great White Fleet
Flag Commander: Rear Admiral Robley D. Evans*
Flagship: USS Connecticut

First Battleship Squadron: Rear Admiral Robley D. Evans

First Battleship Division

Rear Admiral Robley D. Evans:
USS Connecticut (BB-18)
USS Kansas (BB-21)
USS Vermont (BB-20)
USS Louisiana (BB-19)

Second Battleship Division

Rear Admiral William H. Emory:
USS Georgia (BB-15)
USS New Jersey (BB-16)
USS Rhode Island (BB-17)
USS Virginia (BB-13)

Second Battleship Squadron: Rear Admiral Charles M. Thomas

Third Battleship Division

Rear Admiral Charles M. Thomas:
USS Minnesota (BB-22)
USS Ohio (BB-12)
USS Missouri (BB-11)
USS Maine (BB-10)

Fourth Battleship Division

Rear Admiral Charles S. Sperry:
USS Alabama (BB-08)
USS Illinois (BB-07)
USS Kearsarge (BB-05)
USS Kentucky (BB-06)

- Rear Admiral Evans was in ill-health at the start of the voyage. His condition deteriorated as the voyage progressed. Admiral Evans was detached from Connecticut on April 1, 1908, and officially relieved from duty on May 9. Rear Admiral Charles M. Thomas assumed command, but only for six days. Thomas was due to retire in October and he had a heart condition. Admiral Thomas died less than two months later from a heart attack. Rear Admiral Charles Stillman Sperry transferred his flag to *Connecticut* on May 15, 1908, as the third and final commander of the Great White Fleet. Rear Admiral William H. Emory assumed command of Second Battleship Squadron. The resulting vacancies were filled by Captain Seaton Schroeder of *Virginia* and Captain Richard Wainwright of *Louisiana*. Both men were elevated to flag rank.

- Prior to the Great White Fleet's departure from San Francisco for the Pacific leg of the voyage, battleships *Maine* and *Alabama* were replaced by *Nebraska* and *Wisconsin*. *Maine* was replaced due to her inordinate appetite for coal. *Alabama* was sidelined for a cracked cylinder head.

SPECIFICATIONS AND OPERATIONAL HISTORIES
OF BATTLESHIPS OF THE CONNECTICUT CLASS

BB-18 USS CONNECTICUT

- **Authorized:** July 1, 1902.
- **Keel Laid:** March 10, 1903.
- **Launched:** September 29, 1904.
- **Commissioned:** September 29, 1906.
- **Sponsor:** Miss Alice Welles.
- **Standard Displacement:** 16,000 tons.
- **Full Load Displacement:** 17,650 tons.
- **Designed Crew Complement:** 42 officers, 785 enlisted, total 827 men. Total 916 as flagship.
- **Construction Cost:** $6,340,247.63.
- **Builder:** New York Navy Yard, Brooklyn, New York.
- **Armament:** Four 12-inch (305mm) 45 caliber. Capacity: 60 rounds per gun. Weight of projectile: 870 pounds. Muzzle velocity: 2,850 feet-per-second. Range: 15,000 yards. Eight 8-inch (203mm) 45 caliber. Capacity: 100 rounds per gun. Weight of projectile: 260 pounds. Muzzle velocity: 2,700 feet-per-second. Range: 12,000 yards.
- Twelve 7-inch 45 caliber; twenty 3-inch 50 caliber;

twelve 3- pounder; four 1-pounder; four .30 caliber machine guns; four 21-inch submerged torpedo tubes.

- **Armor:** 9"-11" main belt; 8"-12" turrets.
- **Machinery:** Vertical triple expansion engines, 4 cylinders, reciprocating. Babcock and Wilcox boilers. Two reciprocating screws.
- Fuel: Coal. Bunker capacity: 2,249 tons. Designed shaft horsepower: 16,500. Designed speed: 18 knots.
- **Overall Length:** 456' 4"; Beam: 76' 10"; Mean Draught: 24' 6".

OPERATIONAL HISTORY, BB-18

- **Laid down:** Brooklyn Navy Yard, March 10, 1903.
- **Launched:** September 29, 1904.
- **Commissioned:** September 29, 1906.
- Flagship of the Atlantic Fleet, April 16, 1907
- Presidential Fleet Review.
- Participated in the opening ceremonies of the Jamestown Exposition, 1907.
- Flagship of President Theodore Roosevelt's Great White Fleet: The Great White Fleet departed Hampton Roads, Virginia, on December 16, 1907. Fleet sailed round the world for a total of 46,729 miles. Returned to Hampton Roads on February 22, 1909.

- **Objective:** The circumnavigation of the globe in a peacetime demonstration of American naval power.
- Flagship of the Atlantic Fleet until 1912:
  European cruise, November 2, 1910 to March 17, 1911.
- Assigned to the Fourth Battleship Division, Atlantic Fleet, 1913-1915: BB-18 frequently flagship of Fourth Battleship Division.
- Flagship of the Fifth Battleship Division, Atlantic Fleet.
- **World War I:** Based in York River, Virginia. Training of gun crews and midshipmen in Chesapeake Bay.
- Troop transport duty, to and from Brest, France, January 6, 1919 to June 22, 1919.
- Flagship of the Second Battleship Squadron, Atlantic Fleet, June 23, 1919.
- Midshipman cruise, Caribbean, 1920.
- Midshipman cruise, Europe, 1921.
- Assigned as Flagship Training, Pacific Fleet, August 21, 1921.
- Final cruise, San Pedro to Puget Sound, December 16, 1922.
- Sold for scrap, November 1, 1923, under the terms of the Washington Naval Treaty of February 8, 1922.

BB-19 USS LOUISIANA

- **Authorized:** July 1, 1902.
- **Keel Laid:** February 7, 1903.
- **Launched:** August 27, 1904.
- **Commissioned:** June 2, 1906.
- **Sponsor:** Miss Juanita Laland.
- **Standard Displacement:** 16,000 tons.
- **Full Load Displacement:** 17,650 tons.
- **Designed Crew Complement:** 42 officers, 785 enlisted, total 827 men. Total 916 as flagship.
- **Builder:** Newport News Shipbuilding Company, Newport News, Virginia.
- **Armament:** Four 12-inch (305mm) 45 caliber. Capacity: 60 rounds per gun. Weight of projectile: 870 pounds. Muzzle velocity: 2,850 feet-per-second. Range: 15,000 yards. Eight 8-inch (203mm) 45 caliber. Capacity: 100 rounds per gun. Weight of projectile: 260 pounds. Muzzle velocity: 2,700 feet-per-second. Range: 12,000 yards. Twelve 7-inch 45 caliber; twenty 3-inch 50 caliber; twelve 3-pounder; two 1-pounder; four 21-inch submerged torpedo tubes.
- **Armor:** 9"-11" main belt; 8"-12" turrets.
- **Machinery:** Vertical triple expansion engines, 4 cylinders, reciprocating. Babcock and Wilcox boilers. Two

reciprocating screws. Fuel: Coal. Bunker capacity: 2,376 tons. Designed shaft horsepower: 16,500. Designed speed: 18 knots.

- **Overall Length:** 456' 4"; Beam: 76' 10"; Mean Draught: 24' 6".

OPERATIONAL HISTORY, BB-19

- **Laid down:** Newport News, Virginia, February 7, 1903.
- **Launched:** August 27, 1904.
- **Commissioned:** June 2, 1906.
- Lifted William H. Taft and Robert Bacon to Havana to attend the Peace Commission, November 8, 1906.
- Assigned to the Great White Fleet, December 16, 1907 to February 22, 1909.
- Assigned to the Second Battleship Division, Atlantic Fleet, November 1, 1910.
- Assigned to Mexican waters for the protection of American lives and property and enforcement of the Monroe Doctrine, July 6, 1913 to September 24, 1915.
- **World War I:** Assigned to Norfolk, Virginia: Reserve fleet and training vessel for midshipmen. Gunnery and engineering training vessel.

- September 1918, convoy escort, Halifax, Nova Scotia.
- Decommissioned at the Philadelphia Navy Yard, October 20, 1920.
- Assigned for scrap, November 1, 1923.

BB-20 USS VERMONT

- **Authorized:** March 3, 1903.
- **Keel Laid:** May 21, 1904.
- **Launched:** August 31, 1905.
- **Commissioned:** March 4, 1907.
- **Sponsor:** Miss Jennie Bell.
- **Standard Displacement:** 16,000 tons.
- **Full Load Displacement:** 17,650 tons.
- **Designed Crew Complement:** 42 officers, 838 enlisted, total 880 men. Total 916 as flagship.
- **Builder:** Fore River Shipbuilding Company, Quincy, Massachusetts.
- **Armament:** Four 12-inch (305mm) 45 caliber. Capacity: 60 rounds per gun. Weight of projectile: 870 pounds. Muzzle velocity: 2,850 feet-per-second. Range: 15,000 yards. Eight 8-inch (203mm) 45 caliber. Capacity: 100 rounds per gun. Weight of projectile: 260 pounds. Muzzle velocity: 2,700 feet-per-second. Range: 12,000

yards. Twelve 7-inch 45 caliber; twenty 3-inch 50 caliber; ten 3-pounder; two 1-pounder; six .30 caliber machine guns; four 21-inch submerged torpedo tubes.

- **Armor:** 9" main belt; 8"-12" turrets.
- **Machinery:** Vertical triple expansion engines, 4 cylinders, reciprocating. Babcock and Wilcox boilers. Two reciprocating screws. Fuel: Coal. Bunker capacity: 2,405 tons. Designed shaft horsepower: 16,500. Designed speed: 18 knots.
- **Overall Length:** 456' 4"; Beam: 76' 10"; Mean Draught: 24' 6".

OPERATIONAL HISTORY, BB-20

- **Laid down:** Quincy, Massachusetts, May 21, 1904.
- **Launched:** August 31, 1905.
- **Commissioned:** March 4, 1907.
- Shakedown cruise. Assigned to the First Battleship Division, Atlantic Fleet, 1907.
- Assigned to the Great White Fleet, December 16, 1907 to February 22, 1909.
- Assigned to the Atlantic Fleet, 1910-1917: April 1914, Vera Cruz, Mexico, for the protection of American lives and property and enforcement of the Monroe Doctrine.

- Assigned to Chesapeake Bay as an engineering training vessel, August 1917 to November 1918.
- Assigned to troop transport duty, to and from Europe, January-June 1919.
- Assigned to Mare Island, California, September 18, 1919, for inactive status.
- Decommissioned on June 30, 1920.
- Struck from the Navy roster, November 11, 1923. Sold as scrap, November 30, 1923, to meet the terms of the Washington Naval Treaty of February 8, 1922.

BB-21 USS KANSAS

- **Authorized:** March 3, 1903.
- **Keel Laid:** February 10, 1904.
- **Launched:** August 12, 1905.
- **Commissioned:** April 18, 1907.
- **Sponsor:** Miss Anna Hoch.
- **Standard Displacement:** 16,000 tons.
- **Full Load Displacement:** 17,650 tons.
- **Designed Crew Complement:** 42 officers, 838 enlisted, total 880 men. Total 916 as flagship.
- **Builder:** New York Shipbuilding Corporation, Camden, New Jersey.
- **Armament:** Four 12-inch (305mm) 45 caliber.

Capacity: 60 rounds per gun. Weight of projectile: 870 pounds. Muzzle velocity: 2,850 feet-per-second. Range: 15,000 yards. Eight 8-inch (203mm) 45 caliber. Capacity: 100 rounds per gun. Weight of projectile: 260 pounds. Muzzle velocity: 2,700 feet-per-second. Range: 12,000 yards. Twelve 7-inch 45 caliber; twenty 3-inch 50 caliber; twelve 3 pounder; two 1-pounder; two .30 caliber machine guns; four 21-inch submerged torpedo tubes.

* **Armor:** 9" main belt; 8"-12" turrets.
* **Machinery:** Vertical triple expansion engines, 4 cylinders, reciprocating. Babcock and Wilcox boilers. Two reciprocating screws. Fuel: Coal. Bunker capacity: 2,310 tons. Designed shaft horsepower: 16,500. Designed speed: 18 knots.

* **Overall Length:** 456' 4"; Beam: 76' 10"; Mean Draught: 24' 6".

OPERATIONAL HISTORY, BB-21

* **Laid down:** Camden, New Jersey, February 10, 1904.
* **Launched:** August 12, 1905.
* **Commissioned:** April 18, 1907.
* Assigned to the Great White Fleet, December 16, 1907 to February 22, 1909.

- Assigned to the Second Battleship Division, Atlantic Fleet, April 1910: Midshipman cruise. To Italy, 1913.
- Assigned to the Fourth Battleship Division, Atlantic Fleet, April 1917.
- Assigned to Chesapeake Bay for World War I as an engineering training vessel.
- Assigned to transport duty between U.S. and Brest, France, following German capitulation.
- 1920: Cruises to Honolulu, Seattle, San Francisco and San Pedro. Assigned to Second Battleship Squadron, Fourth Battleship Division, Pacific Fleet, as flagship for Rear Admiral Hughes.
- June to September 1921, cruises to Norway, Portugal, Gibraltar and Guantanamo Bay.
- Decommissioned at the Philadelphia Navy Yard, December 16, 1921. Stricken from the Navy roster, August 24, 1923 and sold for scrap according to the terms of the Washington Naval Treaty of February 8, 1922.

BB-22 USS MINNESOTA

- **Authorized:** March 3, 1903.
- **Keel Laid:** October 27, 1903.
- **Launched:** April 8, 1905.
- **Commissioned:** March 9, 1907.
- **Sponsor:** Miss Rose Marie Schaller.
- **Standard Displacement:** 16,000 tons.
- **Full Load Displacement:** 17,650 tons.
- **Designed Crew Complement:** 42 officers, 838 enlisted, total 880 men. 916 total as flagship.
- **Builder:** Newport News Shipbuilding Company, Newport News, Virginia.
- **Armament:** Four 12-inch (305mm) 45 caliber. Capacity: 60 rounds per gun. Weight of projectile: 870 pounds. Muzzle velocity: 2,850 feet-per-second. Range: 15,000 yards. Eight 8-inch (203mm) 45 caliber. Capacity: 100 rounds per gun. Weight of projectile: 260 pounds. Muzzle velocity: 2,700 feet-per-second. Range: 12,000 yards. Twelve 7-inch 45 caliber; twenty 3-inch 50 caliber; twelve 3-pounder; two 1-pounder; two .30 caliber machine guns; four 21-inch submerged torpedo tubes.
- **Armor:** 9" main belt; 8"-12" turrets.
- **Machinery:** Vertical triple expansion engines, 4 cyl-

inders, reciprocating. Babcock and Wilcox boilers. Two reciprocating screws. Fuel: Coal. Bunker capacity: 2,387 tons. Designed shaft horsepower: 16,500. Designed speed: 18 knots.

- Overall Length: 456' 4"; Beam: 76' 10"; Mean Draught: 24' 6".

Operational History, bb-22

- **Laid down:** Newport News, Virginia, October 27, 1903.
- **Launched:** April 8, 1905.
- **Commissioned:** March 9, 1907.
- Assigned to the Great White Fleet, December 16, 1907 to February 22, 1909.
- Assigned to the Fourth Battleship Division, Atlantic Fleet.

- World War I: Assigned as a training vessel for engineering and gunnery. Struck a mine sowed by U-117 off the U.S. coast on September 29, 1917. Minor damage to starboard side.

- Assigned to transport duty between U.S. and France, March-July 1919.

- Final posting as a training vessel, July 1919 to November

1921. Decommissioned on December 1, 1921. Scrapped at the Philadelphia Navy Yard, January 23, 1924.

BB-25 NEW HAMPSHIRE

- **Authorized:** April 27, 1904.
- **Keel Laid:** May 1, 1905.
- **Launched:** June 30, 1906.
- **Commissioned:** March 19, 1908.
- **Sponsor:** Miss Hazel E. Stone.
- **Standard Displacement:** 16,000 tons.
- **Full Load Displacement:** 17,650 tons.
- **Designed Crew Complement:** 41 officers, 809 enlisted, total 850 men.
- **Builder:** New York Shipbuilding Corporation, Camden, New Jersey.
- **Armament:** Four 12-inch (305mm) 45 caliber. Capacity: 60 rounds per gun. Weight of projectile: 870 pounds. Muzzle velocity: 2,850 feet-per-second. Range: 15,000 yards. Eight 8-inch (203mm) 45 caliber. Capacity: 100 rounds per gun. Weight of projectile: 260 pounds. Muzzle velocity: 2,700 feet-per-second. Range: 12,000 yards. Twelve 7-inch 45 caliber; twenty

3-inch 50 caliber; two 1-pounder; two .30 caliber machine guns; four 21-inch submerged torpedo tubes.

- **Armor:** 9" main belt; 8"-12" turrets.
- **Machinery:** Vertical triple expansion engines, 4 cylinders, reciprocating. Babcock and Wilcox boilers. Two reciprocating screws. Fuel: Coal. Bunker capacity: 2,287 tons. Designed shaft horsepower: 16,500. Designed speed: 18 knots: Overall Length: 456' 4"; Beam: 76' 10"; Mean Draught: 24' 6".

OPERATIONAL HISTORY, BB-25

- **Laid down:** Camden, New Jersey, April 27, 1904.
- **Launched:** June 30, 1906.
- **Commissioned:** March 19, 1908.
- Assigned to escort duty, Marine Expeditionary Force, Panama, June 1908.
- Assigned to the Naval Review for the return of the Great White Fleet, Hampton Roads, February 22, 1909.
- Assigned to the Atlantic Fleet, 1909.
- Assigned to the Second Battleship Division, Atlantic Fleet. Cruises to Great Britain, France, Germany and Russia, 1910.
- Midshipman cruises, 1912 and 1913.

- Ordered to Vera Cruz, Mexico, April 1914.
- Ordered to Santo Domingo, December 1916.
- World War I: Assigned as a gunnery and engineering training vessel. Convoy duty, September-December 1918.
- Assigned to troop transport duty, to and from U.S. and France, December 1918 to June 1919.
- Assigned to Haiti, October 1920 to January 1921. Lifted Swedish minister to Sweden, returned to Philadelphia, January-March 1921.
- Decommissioned at the Philadelphia Navy Yard, May 21, 1921. Sold for scrap, November 1, 1923, in accordance with the terms of the Washington Naval Treaty of February 8, 1922.

COMMEMORATION DAY, BATTLESHIP CONNECTICUT

On May 25, 2005, Senator Robert Duff of Connecticut's 25th Senate District, Representative Chris Perone of Connecticut's 137th Assembly District and I commemorated the centennial of the battleship *Connecticut* before both houses of government in Hartford. I cannot thank these two men enough, especially Senator Duff and senatorial assistant Dean O'Brien, for taking the time out of their busy schedules to commemorate USS *Connecticut*. I would also like to thank them for awarding me a General Assembly Citation for my efforts in remembering an important event in Connecticut history. Like this book, I dedicate that citation to the officers and men of battleship *Connecticut.*

Below are the remarks I penned for Senator Robert Duff for the commemoration exercise before the Senate. First are the introductory remarks, followed by the remarks of importance:

Remarks of Introduction

Today we commemorate the centennial of the battleship *Connecticut.* Battleship *Connecticut* was the fourth man-of-war to represent the Constitution State on the Navy roster. Like her illustrious predecessors, battleship *Connecticut* served her country nobly in peacetime and in war.

Remarks of Importance

One hundred years ago, no other American battleship was bigger, faster and more powerful than battleship *Connecticut.* She was the lead ship of a class of six, the largest single class of battleships ever built by the United States. Her distinctive career is evidenced by her accomplishments: Flagship Fourth Battleship Division, Atlantic Fleet; Flagship Fifth Battleship Division, Atlantic Fleet; Flagship Second Battleship Squadron, Atlantic Fleet; Flagship Atlantic Fleet, twice; Flagship Training, Pacific Fleet. But the greatest honor accorded USS

Connecticut was flagship of President Theodore Roosevelt's Great White Fleet. Sixteen battleships departed Hampton Roads on December 16, 1907, and returned to Hampton Roads on February 22, 1909. The round-the-world cruise proved a milestone in modern maritime history; a remarkable 46,000 mile odyssey in an extraordinary peacetime demonstration of naval power. An enterprise that forever altered world history by establishing the United States as a global power; an endeavor led from start to finish by battleship *Connecticut.*

Perhaps the legacy of battleship *Connecticut* is best summed up by Theodore Roosevelt. For upon the fleet's return, on George Washington's Birthday in 1909, the president came aboard the intrepid battleship. And to her captain and crew, he said, "Other nations may do as you have done, but they'll have to follow you."

State of Connecticut

QUI TRANSTULIT SUSTINET

General Assembly
Official Citation

Introduced by Sen. Bob Duff, 25th Dist.   Rep. Chris Perone, 137th Dist.
Rep. Joseph Mann, 140th Dist.   Rep. John J. Ryan,141st Dist.
Rep. Lawrence F. Cafero, Jr., 142nd Dist.   Rep. Antonietta Boucher, 143rd Dist.

Be it hereby known to all that:
The Connecticut General Assembly
hereby offers its sincerest congratulations to:

Mark Albertson

In recognition of

Your deep interest in the USS Connecticut.
As we mark the centennial of this grand and historic battleship,
the entire General Assembly thanks you for your continued efforts to
educate others about the State of Connecticut's place in world history.

The entire membership extends its
very best wishes on this memorable occasion
and expresses the hope for continued success.

Given this 2nd day of May 2005
at the State Capitol
Hartford, Connecticut

by

President Pro Tempore

Speaker of the House

Secretary of the State

PART FOUR

USS Connecticut steaming at high speed off the coast of Maine, 1907.
Photographed by Enrique Muller, whose boat was nearly swamped by
the battleship's wake. Courtesy, Naval Historical Center, NH553

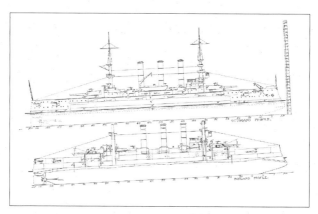

Outboard and inboard profiles of USS Connecticut.
Courtesy, Naval Historical Center, NH6655

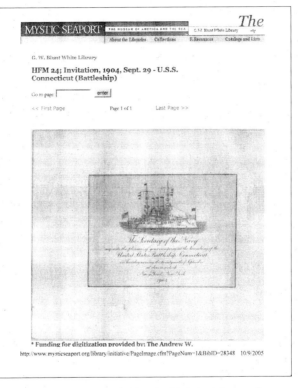

Invitation to the launching of USS Connecticut at the Brooklyn Navy Yard on September 29, 1904. Courtesy, © Mystic Seaport Collection, Mystic, Conn. #1951.3976

*Launching of USS Connecticut at the Brooklyn Navy Yard
on September 29, 1904. 30,000 people turned out to watch
America's newest battleship slide down the building ways.
Courtesy, Naval Historical Center, NH94970-KN*

*September 7, 1906. USS Connecticut fitting out in dry dock
number 3 at the Brooklyn Navy Yard not long before the ship's
commissioning. Courtesy, Naval Historical Center, 19-N-4-25-3*

USS Connecticut on the day she was commissioned into
the fleet at the Brooklyn Navy Yard, September 29, 1906.
Courtesy, Naval Historical Center, 19-N-4-25-33

Gun crew from the after 12-inch gun turret, USS
Connecticut, 1906. Photo was colorized as a post card.
Courtesy, Naval Historical Center, NH101253-KN

*USS Connecticut departing New York City, December 15,
1906. Courtesy, Naval Historical Center, NH55334*

*USS Connecticut leading the Great White Fleet out of Hampton
Roads, December 16, 1907, at the start of the round-the-world
cruise. Courtesy, Naval Historical Center, NH100349*

**President Roosevelt reviewing the Battle Fleet at the time
of its world cruise**

The above is **President Roosevelt** addressing all of the Captains prior
to our departure for the Pacific Coast, as our Country was on the verg
of war with Japan over California. He told them "If Japan intends to
make war, I want to be prepared. I do not propose to have anyone
'pull a gun' on me and tell me to throw up my hands. " He told his
officers if war came and any commander lost his ship because he was
surprised or unprepared, he might just as well never come home
himself. His last words to Admiral Evans were "You know what to do
if war comes. "

President Theodore Roosevelt reviewing the Great White

Fleet from aboard USS Connecticut, December 16, 1907.

To the president's right is Rear Admiral Charles S. Sperry.

Courtesy, Naval Historical Center, NH67142

USS Connecticut at anchor in Callao, 1908. Peru was one of the most successful visits made by the Great White Fleet during the round-the-world cruise, Courtesy, Naval Historical Center, NH001571

USS Connecticut in San Diego during the round-the-world cruise, 1908. Courtesy, Naval Historical Center, NH73318

USS Connecticut leading the Great White Fleet into San Francisco Bay, May 6, 1908. Courtesy, Naval Historical Center, NH59537

Many animals were picked up along the way during the round-the-world cruise. Here a bluejacket on Connecticut feeds a bear that was picked up at Bremerton, Washington, 1908. Courtesy, Naval Historical Center, NH50481

This kangaroo was presented to the Connecticut by the citizens of Sydney, Australia, 1908. Feeding the long-eared crewman is Lt. John E. Lewis. Courtesy, Naval Historical Center, NH50477

Lifeboat drill for crewmembers of USS Connecticut during the round-the-world cruise. Courtesy, Naval Historical Center, NH001748

Sailors at play on the after deck of USS Connecticut. Note
other ships of the Great White Fleet steaming astern.
Courtesy, Naval Historical Center, NH42757

Gun crews from Connecticut's 7-inch guns poking their heads through
the holes in their targets following gunnery practice, at Magdalena
Bay, Mexico, 1908. Courtesy, Naval Historical Center, NH60991

USS Connecticut at Messina, Italy during the round-the-world cruise, January 1909. Connecticut (on the right) was on hand to render assistance following the massive earthquake, which had devastated southern Italy. Courtesy, Naval Historical Center, NH1570

President Theodore Roosevelt addressing the crew of USS Connecticut upon the ship's return from the round-the-world cruise, February 22, 1909. As flagship of the Great White Fleet, Connecticut had steamed a remarkable 46,729 miles. Courtesy, Naval Historical Center, NH001836

Battleships of the Atlantic Fleet on the Hudson River off 145th Street in New York City, on hand for the Hudson-Fulton Celebration. At anchor from left to right are, Louisiana, Idaho, Kansas, Vermont and Connecticut. Connecticut was the host ship for the festivities, October 1909. Courtesy, Naval Historical Center, NH91471

The business end of USS Connecticut's after 12-inch guns, 1910. Note the pole masts in the background. This photo was taken just prior to the changeover to the cage masts. Courtesy, Naval Historical Center, 19-N-60-10-3

The tremendous muzzle flash of USS Connecticut's 8-inch guns, 1913. Courtesy, Naval Historical Center, NH63640

A stern of USS Connecticut while in dry dock, 1914. Note the propellers, rudder and the ship's armor belt along the hull. Courtesy, Naval Historical Center, NH73787

USS Connecticut 1914. Note the cage masts. All six ships of the Connecticut class had their cage masts installed during the 1910–11 refit. Courtesy, Naval Historical Center, NH43114

Battleships of the Connecticut class steaming in formation during Atlantic Fleet exercises, circa, 1914–15. Ship nearest to the camera is USS Connecticut. Courtesy, Naval Historical Center, NH95154

The crew was mustered for a photograph while USS
Connecticut was in the Philadelphia Navy Yard, 1919.
Courtesy, Naval Historical Center, NH82523

USS Connecticut transiting the Panama Canal, 1920. Note the ship's clock
at the base of the cage mast. Courtesy, Naval Historical Center, NH73813

USS Connecticut in Honolulu, 1922. Courtesy,
Naval Historical Center, NH83084

USS Connecticut in the shipyard for scrapping, 1924. The scars of the
cutter's torch are evident. Courtesy, Naval Historical Center, NH55347

USS Connecticut as featured on a U.S. Navy recruiting poster,

1932. Courtesy, Naval Historical Center, NH55333

BIBLIOGRAPHY

Books:

Friedman, Norman, **U.S.** *Battleships,* Naval Institute Press, Annapolis, MD., 1985.

Newhart, Max, *American Battleships,* Pictorial Histories Publishing Co. Inc.,Missoula, Montana, 1995.

Reckner, James R., *Great White Fleet,* Naval Institute Press, Annapolis, MD., 1988.

Weapons and Warfare, vol. 6, Columbia House, New York City, 1967.

Weapons and Warfare, vol. 21, Columbia House, New York City, 1967.

Periodicals & Newspapers:

Albertson, Mark, "When Connecticut led the Great White Fleet," *Connecticut Post,* October 10, 2004.

Strait, Raymond, "The Cage Mast Fleet," *Battleships at War!* SEA CLASSICS Magazine Special, Fall 1984.

Government Sources:

Navy Department, Office of the Chief of Naval Operations, Division of Naval History(09 09B9) Ships' Histories Section, *History of Ships Named Connecticut.*